W9-CIQ-486

THE BIBLE IN CHRISTIAN TEACHING

ALETHEIA Paperbacks now available
for your individual or group study:

An Adventure in Love
W. Taliaferro Thompson
Adventures in Parenthood
W. Taliaferro Thompson
The Bible in Christian Teaching
Holmes Rolston
A Call to Faith
Rachel Henderlite
The Creative Era
Carl G. Howie
The Enduring Message of the Bible
L. Harold DeWolf
Faces About the Christ
Holmes Rolston
Forgiveness and Hope
Rachel Henderlite
The Gospel According to Mark and Its Meaning for Today
Ernest Trice Thompson
Handbook for Christian Believers
A. J. Ungersma
In the Beginning God
William M. Logan
The Nature and Mission of the Church
Donald G. Miller
Out of the Whirlwind
William B. Ward
Reasons for Our Faith
Henry T. Close
The Revelation of Jesus Christ
Donald W. Richardson
Scripture and the Christian Response
Howard Tillman Kuist
The Sermon on the Mount and Its Meaning for Today
Ernest Trice Thompson
The Story of the Reformation
William Stevenson
Understanding the Books of the New Testament
edited by Patrick H. Carmichael
Understanding the Books of the Old Testament
edited by Patrick H. Carmichael
We Believe
Henry Wade DuBose

THE BIBLE IN CHRISTIAN TEACHING

BY HOLMES ROLSTON

UNITY SCHOOL LIBRARY
DISCARD
Lee's Summit, Missouri 64063

JOHN KNOX PRESS
Richmond, Virginia

Library of Congress Catalog Card Number: 62-10238

Aletheia Edition 1966

Second printing 1967

Unless otherwise noted, Scripture quotations are from the Revised Standard Version, copyright 1946 and 1952 by Division of Christian Education of the National Council of the Churches of Christ in the United States of America.

© M. E. Bratcher 1962
Printed in the United States of America
37-3130

BT
89
R6

Dedicated to the members of the
Staff of the Board of Christian Education
who are working together to produce the
Covenant Life Curriculum of the
Presbyterian Church in the United States
and the
Reformed Church in America.

Preface

THIS BOOK is written against the background of many years of preaching, teaching, writing, and editing in which my central concern has been to understand the message of the Bible and to present this message in its relevance for life today. Here, it has been my intent to make explicit that which has been implicit in my approach to the Bible during the whole of my ministry. I have done this in the hope that my labors in the years to come may be enriched by this statement of my convictions concerning the Bible's place in Christian teaching. This book is written in the hope that my thinking concerning the significance of the Bible in the church's educational task may be helpful to others who are also seeking to give their Christian witness to our generation.

HOLMES ROLSTON

Contents

 I

The Indispensable Book

Revelation Event and Written Word

THE BIBLE is a very ancient book. Why then is it given so significant a role in religious education in the modern world? No one would think today of using a textbook in physics that was not of recent origin. A textbook in psychology which was used in our colleges a few decades ago would be very much out of date for the teaching of psychology today. It is true that in the realm of literature or of philosophy we find much of value in the work of the past. Homer's Iliad is still a great poem. The dialogues of Plato make valuable reading in the modern world. But such books would be studied in courses in the history of literature or philosophy. They would not be at the center of a curriculum. We may be interested in a study of the religious beliefs of the ancient Egyptians, but it would be ridiculous to suggest that such a study would give the clue to the meaning of life in the twentieth century. Why then are we so concerned in Christian teaching today with the story of how the children of Israel went out of the land of Egypt?

The man who is not a Christian cannot help wondering why those who teach in the church school consider the study of the Bible so crucial for the communication of their faith today. In fact, the questions that are raised concerning the place of the Bible in the teaching ministry of the church are not limited to those who are not professing Christians. Many of those who have joined our churches find, when they open the pages of their Bible, that they are in an entirely different world from the one in which they now live. The Bible comes out of a world which is in many respects different from the world of the twentieth century.

The coming of the industrial revolution has left us with an

interdependent economic order which has little in common with the simple pastoral and agricultural society that provides the setting of the narrative of the Bible. We live today in a world of automobiles and radios and television. We have entered the age of atomic energy. We stand on the verge of space travel. Our knowledge of the world in which we live has left us with an understanding of the nature of the physical universe which is quite different from the way the writers of the Bible thought of earth and sea and sky.

We live in a world of science which assumes in the physical universe a relation of cause and effect that leaves little room for the supernatural. It is against the background of our understanding of the life of the modern world that we are bound to inquire about the relevance of the Bible for life today. Can a book written over a period of nearly fifteen hundred years, with its most ancient writings nearly three thousand years old and with its most recent portions written more than eighteen hundred years ago, be indispensable for the thought and life of the modern world? Can a book originally written in Hebrew or Aramaic or Greek be vital to the life of the English-speaking world?

If we would ask the average church school teacher why the Bible is important for Christian teaching, we would probably be told that this book is indispensable because it is the Word of God. The answer would be correct, but it would need to be defined. The Bible comes to us as a written record from the life of the people of God in various ages and points beyond itself to the way in which God has made himself known in human history. An atheist would insist that we cannot have a valid revelation of God. He would deny that there is any such thing in history as revelation; but those who stand within the fellowship of the Christian church believe that the God who made them has not left them in complete ignorance of what they should believe concerning him or of the duty which he requires of them. They believe that God at various times and places and in different ways has spoken to us through the prophets (Hebrews 1:1). They believe also that God has made himself known to man in the life and death and resurrection of Jesus Christ. They believe that in Jesus Christ the Word has become flesh and dwelt among us. And they are convinced that the Bible is the indispensable book because they find in the Bible the written record that points beyond itself to the revelation of himself which God has given to man.

Revelation Event

If we are to understand the peculiar significance of the Bible as the written word, we must understand the nature of the revelation events to which the Bible bears witness. In the effort to distinguish the revelation event from other events in the stream of history, we may say that a revelation event is an incident experienced by one or more persons in which and through which the direct action of God himself is recognized. In such events persons are brought to an awareness of God, his attributes or actions, which they often judge to be previously unknown (at least to themselves); thus, such events may be described as "revelation events." The Old and New Testaments provide for us a continuous sequence of such events in which a succession of persons received a series of related communications from the same one God. The revelation which God gives of himself culminates in the event of the coming of the Christ, i.e., that which God has said through the sending of his Son to us.

The clearest example that we have of revelation event is the resurrection of Jesus Christ from the dead. As we contemplate the supreme mystery of the resurrection of our Lord, we can mark some of the characteristics of revelation events. We have here both history and what may be called holy history. The Resurrection is history. It is an event. It happens at a definite time—on the third day after the Crucifixion. It takes place in the tomb of Joseph. The tomb is empty, and the risen Lord manifests himself alive to his disciples. With the Resurrection we have the beginning of a stream of events which profoundly affect human history. The Resurrection is also "holy history." It cannot be explained in terms of cause and effect. It is an act of God. The secular historian can affirm as a fact of history the appearance of a fellowship of people who witnessed to the empty tomb and to the risen Lord. He cannot explain it in terms of cause and effect;

he is not qualified to deal in purely secular terms with the fact of the Resurrection.

The witness to the revelation event cannot be separated from the belief that the event actually happened. Paul can say that if Christ has not been raised he, Paul, is found to be a false witness of God because he has consistently testified that God raised Christ from the dead (1 Corinthians 15:15).

In revelation event, we have both the actual event and the understanding of it that is found in the believing community. The revelation of Jesus Christ was not an isolated marvel. The first Christians understood the whole life of Jesus in the light of the Resurrection. It was to them God's declaration with power that Jesus was the Son of God. It gave them a fresh insight into the meaning of his death. It enabled them to see the whole life of Jesus in a dimension of depth that would have been impossible apart from the Resurrection.

If the revelation event is filled with meaning for those who stand within the believing fellowship, it is an enigma to those who refuse to receive it. Those who did not accept the witness of the apostles to the resurrection of Jesus were not able to give an adequate explanation to the thing that had happened within the Christian community. This is the enigma which consistently confronts those who deny the reality of revelation event.

While the idea of revelation event is seen most clearly in our study of the Christ event and particularly in our consideration of the Resurrection, it is not limited to the events to which the New Testament bears witness. We have in the history of Israel a series of events through which God made himself known to a people he had chosen to be, in a peculiar way, the instrument of his redemptive purpose for all mankind. This unique series of events begins with the call to Abraham to become the founder of a holy family. We do not know the full details of the revelation of God which was given to such men as Abraham and Isaac and Jacob; but we do know that when the children of Israel went down to Egypt they carried with them a knowledge of God and a sense of destiny. If they had not had something to mark them as unique, the descendents of Jacob who settled in Egypt would soon have become merged in the larger stream of Egyptian life.

Though the sons of Jacob carried a knowledge of God with them when they went to Egypt, it was the Exodus experience that the children of Israel considered crucial for God's revelation of himself to his people. The God who made himself known to Moses reveals himself as the God of Abraham, Isaac, and Jacob. In the deliverance from Egypt he reveals his faithfulness to his covenant with Abraham, his compassion for his people, and his power to deliver them. In the revelation that is given through Moses, we have the Ten Commandments as the summary of the moral law and as the will of the God of Israel for his people. And in the history of Israel, from the Exodus to the close of the Old Testament canon, we have a series of revelation events in which God makes himself known to his people in the events of their history and in the words of his prophets.

As we think of the revelation of God which precedes the coming of the Christ, special emphasis should be given to the Hebrew prophets. These men appear at various times in the history of Israel. But they have in common the knowledge that they are the bearers to Israel of the Word of her God. In such men as Amos, Hosea, Isaiah, and Jeremiah, God spoke to Israel both in judgment and in mercy. He continues to speak through them to the people of God in all ages. The prophets point consistently beyond themselves to the God who has sent them.

Revelation Event and Written Word

Having discussed the nature of revelation event, we can now consider the relation of revelation event and written word. This can be seen most clearly as we contemplate the way in which the New Testament was written. We have first the appearance in history of the God-man. Jesus does not come in complete isolation from the past. Rather, he comes as the consumation and fulfillment of the revelation that has been given to Israel. With Jesus there is a fresh beginning. With Jesus the eternal Word becomes flesh and dwells among us. The impact of Jesus upon his nation is profound. In the end, he is rejected by the religious leaders of his own people, but he gathers to himself disciples who have come to believe that he is indeed the Christ, the Son of God. The death of Jesus is followed by his resurrection. And on the day of Pentecost there is an outpouring of the Holy Spirit in which the witness of the apostles to the Resurrection is accepted, and a community of those who believe that Jesus is the Christ is called into being in the city in which he had been crucified.

In the beginning, the Christian community did not feel the need of a written word. Peter and the apostles preached the forgiveness of God based upon the redemption that God had wrought out in Jesus Christ. And the preaching of the apostles was normative for the witness of the believing community to its Lord. Under the clear guidance of the Holy Spirit, the church broke through the bounds of Judaism and became a universal community offering the salvation of God through Christ to all who would receive it. When Barnabas and Saul started on their first missionary tour, they did not carry with them a copy of the New Testament. The church existed as a believing fellowship with rapidly growing churches in many centers of the Roman Empire before the New Testament was written in the form in which we now have it.

In time, the necessity for written documents became apparent. There were probably written records of the words and deeds of our Lord in the Christian community from the beginning. There is a tradition that Matthew kept a record of the sayings of Jesus. The first writings to be preserved in the church in their original form are probably some of the letters of Paul to his churches. In these letters we have a priceless witness to the understanding of the meaning of the Christian faith that was to be found in the Christian church within two to three decades of the death of Jesus. It was inevitable, however, that in time the memory of her Lord which was preserved in the life of the church should be written down. The four Gospels preserve for us in written form the witness of the church to the words and deeds of her Lord. The writings which became part of the New Testament were selected because the church found them to be in agreement with her understanding of the person and work of her Lord.

While it is not seen as clearly because it is spread over a much longer period of time, a similar relation between revelation event and written word can be traced in the writings of the Old Testament. The revelation events came first. Through his Word and deed God called into being a Messianic people. And in time the people of Israel found it necessary to give an account of themselves through written documents which witnessed to the events that had called the people of God into being. We have in the Old Testament the literature of a unique people through which they point beyond themselves to the God who has made himself known to them.

The Holy Spirit and the Written Word

When we describe the process by which the Bible came into being, we must not neglect the work of the Holy Spirit. Jesus is God manifest in the flesh. The Holy Spirit is God present with us. As we contemplate the work of the Holy Spirit, we should remember that the Spirit is not a group product generated by the community. He comes to the church from beyond the church. He comes not as power to be manipulated but as Power to be obeyed. He raises up within the community men who speak to the community. But it is not their word which they speak; it is not the community's corporate witness which they speak; it is the Word of God. It is the mission and glory of these spirit-filled men to make the events luminous and revelatory by declaring God's own authoritative interpretation of them. Paul could write: "Now we have received not the spirit of the world, but the Spirit which is from God, that we might understand the gifts bestowed on us by God. And we impart this in words not taught by human wisdom but taught by the Spirit, interpreting spiritual truths to those who possess the Spirit" (1 Corinthians 2:12–13). Similarly, the great prophets of the Old Testament were conscious of being the bearers of the Word of the Lord to their generation. The Spirit of God which called into being the believing community was active also in inspiring the authors of the written word.

The Bible as Norm

We have sought to describe the relation between revelation event and written word. We have considered also the work of the Holy Spirit in inspiring the writers of Scripture. We are now ready to discuss the question: Why is the Bible indispensable for Christian preaching and teaching today? We have seen that the written word comes out of the believing community as part of the witness of this community to the revelation events which called it into being. The church existed in the first few decades of Christian history without the benefit of a written record of her message. Those who had stood closest to Jesus could give their witness of him without dependence on written documents. Paul could check his understanding of the gospel he had received from Jesus Christ with the testimony of Peter, John, and James, the brother of our Lord. But the need for written documents must have arisen very soon; eye witnesses die and an oral tradition cannot be depended upon for accuracy. Soon, there must have been the necessity for distinguishing between true and false teaching. Paul and Barnabas had to appeal to the apostles and elders at Jerusalem for support for their insistence that the Gentiles were to be received into the church without being required to submit to circumcision or asked to keep the law of Moses as a condition of salvation. In the beginning, such questions could be settled by direct appeal to those who could be trusted to reflect the mind of the Lord. But very soon it became necessary to have written records which could be appealed to as authoritative. In such a situation men would turn naturally to the letters of Paul for his understanding of the meaning of the Christian faith and for the way in which he spelled out for his converts the implications of trying to live as a Christian in the midst of the Roman society of the first century. As men were concerned that their teaching should be true to the sound words of the Lord Jesus, they turned inevitably to the church's memory of him which was preserved in the four Gospels. The oral tradition and the written word must have existed alongside of each other. We still have in the church a body of traditions that go back very close to the origin of the church and are considered a valuable source of information concerning the life and work of the church. But the Protestant churches have never been willing to exalt tradition above the written word. As the church moved further from her origin and as the appearance of heresy made it necessary to find some basis for distinguishing between true and false teaching, it was inevitable that the written word should be thought of as containing the norm of Christian proclamation. At the heart of the Protestant Reformation there is the conviction that all Christian teaching must be judged against a norm that can be discovered in the Scriptures. This was Luther's contention at the Diet of Worms:

> Unless I am convicted by Scripture and plain reason—I do not accept the authority of popes and councils, for they have contradicted each other—my conscience is captive to the Word of God. I cannot and I will not recant anything, for to go against conscience is neither right nor safe. God help me. Amen.*

The Protestant Reformation set out to reform a corrupt church through hearing again the Word of the Lord of the church as he speaks to his church through the testimony of the written word.

The Bible as Source

It is but a step from the Bible as rule of faith to the Bible as the source of faith. When it was first written, the New Testament existed as one of the sources of the church's knowledge of her Lord. But as those who had known Jesus in the flesh passed away and as the various traditions concerning him became mixed with error, the written word which had been accepted by the church as authoritative increasingly became the place to which those called to a ministry of teaching in the church must go as the source of their message. While the final fixing of the canon came late in the history of the church, the church must have moved rather quickly to the acceptance of the major books of the New Testament as the source of her message. From the beginning, the apostles and their followers looked to the Old Testament as the source of their knowledge of the way in which God had revealed himself to their fathers. If we are to judge by their quotations from it and their references to it, the Old Testament was the one book that was central for the writers of the New Testament. In

* Roland Bainton, *Here I Stand*, p. 185. Nashville: Abingdon Press, 1950.

time the Scriptures of the Old and New Testaments came to be accepted in the church as the source of her message.

THE BIBLE AS THE ONLY SOURCE

We move one step further when we say that the Bible is our only source for Christian teaching. It is here that we understand the sense in which the Bible is indispensable. All that we actually know today concerning God's revelation of himself in Jesus Christ comes to us from the Bible. There is no dependable witness to Jesus that has come to us from contemporary secular sources. If we did not have the witness of the New Testament to Jesus Christ, we would be in complete ignorance of those events through which the church was called into being. We can learn something of the history of Israel from the study of ancient history. A history of Israel can be written showing that nation's life in the setting of the story of the surrounding nations. We are limited, however, to the written record preserved for us in the Old Testament for our understanding of the revelation events through which the children of Israel were molded into a unique people.

When we say that the Bible is the only source of our knowledge of God's revelation of himself in history, we do not mean to say that the history of the Christian church since the closing of the New Testament canon is unimportant. We can learn much from the impact of the gospel message on the various cultures in which the church has lived. There have been in the lives of the great leaders of the church events which are quite similar to the revelation events witnessed to in Scripture. Consider for example Luther's conversion or Wesley's Aldersgate experience. The experiences of the great leaders of the church are witnesses to that which the living Lord has done in the life of the world. But our knowledge of the meaning of Christ to Augustine or Luther does not add to our knowledge of the Christ event. We must go to the Scripture for our knowledge of that which Jesus said and did and for our knowledge of the way in which the church came into being.

"Christian insight begins with man's knowledge of the Bible informed and illuminated by the Holy Spirit. Therefore in Christian education the Bible is not one concern among many; it is the ground and guide of all concerns, and permeates in various ways the entire enterprise of Christian education." *

The Bible as Instrument

We have thought of the written word as witness to revelation event. We must now think of it as the instrument through which the living Christ is continually calling his church into being. When we study the Scriptures today, we find that they bring us immediately into the fellowship of a community which has a tremendous consciousness of the presence of God. The letters to the Thessalonians, for example, are probably the oldest writings in the New Testament to be preserved for us in the form in which they were actually written. If we will examine the picture that they give of the church at Thessalonica, we will find that there was a God-consciousness among the Thessalonian Christians that is tremendous. In the New Testament as a whole we deal with men who have stood in the presence of the Christ event and are certain that they have seen the light of the knowledge of the glory of God in the face of Jesus Christ. Likewise, the God-consciousness which permeates the whole of the Old Testament is unique in ancient literature.

But we cannot remain long in the presence of those who witness to the activity of God in human history without finding ourselves confronted by the God to whom the Scriptures consistently point. The living Christ uses the witness to him which is found in the New Testament to call men today to acknowledge him as Lord and to become his disciples. We can say of the New Testament as a whole that which John says of his Gospel: The New Testament is written that men may believe that Jesus is the Christ, the Son of God, and that believing they may have life in his name (John 20:31). Jesus speaks to men by the witness of his followers. He makes himself known through the preaching of his church. But this witness today must always be tested by the witness to him

* This sentence is from "The Design for the Curriculum of Christian Education," a tentative paper prepared for the Cooperative Curriculum Project at its meeting December 12–14, 1960, at St. Louis, Missouri. Used by permission.

which is found in the pages of the New Testament. The Bible is the indispensable book because it is the witness to the revelation events through which God has made himself known to man. And the Bible is the indispensable book because it is the effective instrument through which the living Lord is continually calling men and women into fellowship with him as Lord and Saviour.

QUESTIONS

1. Why is it that we demand the most recent textbooks for the study of courses in science or technology but depend on a very ancient book, the Bible, as central for Christian teaching today?

2. How would you answer a Communist if he said that the Bible was a book filled with outworn superstitions that must be discarded if man is to make progress in the modern world?

3. What is there that is unique about the Bible when it is compared with other ancient books?

4. What would be your definition of "revelation event"?

5. What are some of the characteristics of such events that can be seen in the study of the resurrection of Jesus?

6. How does the witness of the Scriptures to revelation events cut across the basic assumptions of the agnostic or the atheist?

7. What are some of the events in the history of Israel before the coming of Christ through which God made himself known to his people?

8. Why was the church in the beginning able to exist without the documents which now make up our New Testament?

9. Why did it become necessary to commit the Christian witness to writing?

10. What is the work of the Holy Spirit in the inspiration of the Scripture?

11. In what sense is the Scripture the norm of Christian teaching? the source of Christian teaching?

12. In what sense is the Scripture our only source for Christian teaching?

13. How does the Scripture become the effective instrument of Christian proclamation?

 II

Treasure in Earthen Vessels and the Transcendent Power of God

The Human Element in the Making of the Scriptures

WHEN WE SAY that the Bible is the indispensable book because it is the Word of God, we must face at once the obvious fact that the Bible is also the word of man. When we seek to discover in the Bible a norm by which all Christian preaching and teaching may be judged, we are forced to realize that we will come to an understanding of this norm only by disciplined study. When Christians start to read the Bible, they are certain to find many things they do not understand. They will discover portions of the Bible that may have had real meaning for the original readers but do not seem to have much meaning for them. Those who go to the Bible to hear the Word of God are apt to experience a sense of disappointment and frustration in the beginning. They may wonder if this ancient book really has any relevance for them or for their society. The recognition that the Scripture is indispensable sharpens our problem of how to go to the Scripture so that we hear the Word of God. It is well for us, therefore, to consider in this chapter some of the difficulties which students of the Bible must face when they seek to understand its message.

THE WORD OF GOD IN THE SPEECH OF MAN

The fundamental difficulty we must always face in any effort to understand the Word of God is the realization that it always comes to us in the words of man. This difficulty is inescapable because it is only as God comes to us in our own language that we can understand him. The coming of God's Word in the speech of man has similar characteristics with the Word that becomes flesh. But when the Word of the Lord is expressed in the language of man, it partakes inevitably of the frailty and the possibility of error which is characteristic of all things human.

An example of this is found in the name of God which is revealed to Moses when he receives his call to deliver the children of Israel from Egypt (Exodus 3:14). The name is spelled with the capital letters YHWH. It is usually pronounced Yahweh. But what does the name mean? It is a form of the Hebrew verb to be (*hayah*). The Revised Standard Version translates the name, I AM WHO I AM. If this translation is correct, the name stands for the transcendent being of God. It expresses the eternal and unchanging nature of God. But in a footnote the R.S.V. tells us that the expression can also be translated I AM WHAT I AM or I WILL BE WHAT I WILL BE. If the latter translation is adopted, God is telling Moses that he will be what he reveals himself to be in the history of his people. The meaning of the name of God will be revealed in his dealings with the covenant nation. The two ideas are not necessarily contradictory. They may supplement each other. This effort to define the meaning of the name of God given to Moses does illustrate, however, the frailty of all human language as the medium of the divine Word.

An illustration of the same principle is found in the study of the Ten Commandments. Suppose, for example, that we had the two tables of stone on which the Ten Commandments were originally written. There would in this case be no question about the accuracy of the text. But we would still have to express the meaning of these commandments in terms of our own life situation. Consider, for example, the commandment: "Thou shalt not kill." We would understand this commandment as a divine word forbidding us to take the life of our fellow man. But we would immediately have to face questions concerning its meaning. Does it prohibit killing in self-defense? Would it mean that there are no circumstances under which a people have the right to wage war? Or consider the commandment: "Thou shalt not commit adultery." This appears to be clear. We would understand that it protects the sanctity of the home. But if we attempted to live by it, we would have to define adultery. Would the commandment forbid polygamy? Would it permit the remarriage of divorced persons? To ask these questions is to realize that no written code can be free from some of the uncertainties always involved in human language.

If we had a written document which had been written by Jesus himself and had been carefully preserved by the church through the ages as an original manuscript in the handwriting of our Lord, we would still have to analyze the meaning of the words and the structure of the sentences. We would probably find that devout Christians differed in some points about the meaning of the document for life today. The demand for a Word of God in the speech of man that does not share in some degree the frailty of all things human is an impossible demand.

The Copying of the Bible

As a part of the human element in the making of the Scriptures, we need to remember that for many centuries the Bible was preserved by copying. We do not have any of the original manuscripts of biblical writings. The oldest complete manuscripts of the New Testament which have been preserved for us are probably to be dated at least three hundred years after the New Testament was written. A much longer time elapsed between the writing of the Old Testament and the date of our earliest Hebrew manuscripts. The manuscripts which we now have of both the New Testament and the Old are copies of copies. This does not mean that the text of the Bible from which translations are now made is not reasonably accurate. Great care was used in copying the text of the Bible. The copy of Isaiah which was discovered in the Dead Sea Scrolls is probably a thousand years older than the oldest complete Hebrew texts of the Old Testament. But the study of the text of Isaiah which was found in these scrolls has helped to confirm the basic integrity of the text we had been using. By comparing different copies, scholars have been able to establish with great accuracy the text of the Bible in its original languages.

No person who understands the way in which the Bible has been copied through the ages would question the necessity for what is called textual criticism. This is the effort of scholars to evaluate carefully the available texts in order to determine as accurately as possible the text of the original manuscripts of Scripture. Any student who will read the footnotes of the R.S.V. will realize the way in which the science of textual criticism has helped us in our knowledge of the text of the Bible.

THE TRANSLATION OF THE BIBLE

If the Bible is to become vital in the lives of people, they must be able to read it in their own language. From this point of view, a vast program of translation has been carried on in which the Bible has been translated from the original languages into all of the major languages of our earth. The thrilling story of this can be learned from the American Bible Society; it is a work which is still being continued as the Bible is being translated in whole or in part into the languages of many smaller groups of people all over the globe. However, our concern here is with the Bible in English. It is not a simple matter for a scholar today to understand the exact meaning of many expressions in the original languages of the Bible and to express this meaning accurately in modern English. An example of this is found in Matthew 20:15 in the closing words of the master to the servants who are protesting his paying of the same wages to all of the laborers. An actual translation into English of the Greek words would be: "Is your eye evil because I am good?" But no one knows just what this means. The R.S.V. translators have rendered it: "Do you begrudge my generosity?" There is not a single English word here that translates a Greek word, but the translators have probably correctly understood the meaning of the phrase. Our modern versions of the Bible are based on a much more accurate text than the text from which the King James translation was made. The principle of seeking continually to translate the Bible into the language which the people actually speak is true to the Protestant principle that the Bible should be given to the people in their own language.

The Thought Forms of the Bible

As we seek to understand the message of the Bible, we need to remember that the Bible is an ancient book that has been preserved by copying and has been translated into modern English. Yet, the difficulties involved in understanding the Bible go deeper than these obvious facts. As part of the human element in the making of the Bible, we need to realize that the writers of the Bible inevitably expressed themselves in the thought forms of their age. We should not be surprised at this.

Consider, for example, the story of Jacob's stealing Esau's blessing (Genesis 27). Underlying this story is the assumption that the blessing of a dying father is irrevocable. We do not believe this, but Isaac believed it and Jacob believed it. Unless we accept this assumption, the story itself has little meaning. But if we understand the way all of the actors of the story feel about the blessing of a dying father, the story moves with the simplicity and power of a Greek tragedy. Consider also Naaman's request for two mules' burden of earth upon which to sacrifice to the Lord. The request may seem strange to us, but to Naaman it was an expression of the conviction that the god of the land had to be worshiped upon his own soil.

Another example of the thought form of the time is found in the language of the second commandment. The children of Israel were forbidden to make themselves "a graven image, or any likeness of anything that is in heaven above, or that is in the earth beneath, or that is in the water under the earth" (Exodus 20:4). We are so familiar with this language that we hardly realize that it assumes the Hebrew understanding of the earth as founded upon the seas. This is clearly stated in the 24th Psalm which begins:

> The earth is the LORD's and the fulness thereof,
> the world and those who dwell therein;
> for he has founded it upon the seas,
> and established it upon the rivers.

We can still believe that the earth is the Lord's because he has created it, even though we would not express this truth in the language that the Hebrew writers used. We can share the concern for the prohibition of all idolatry without accepting the idea of the waters under the earth.

An additional illustration of the difference between the thought forms of the ancient Hebrew world and ours is found in the condemnation of the taking of interest in the Old Testament. The fifteenth Psalm gives a beautiful picture of the man who shall dwell in the holy hill of the Lord. But in the fifth verse he is described as one "who does not put out his money at interest." (The R.S.V. is right in translating this as *interest* and not *usury* as it is in the King James Version.) And Ezekiel in his description of the ideal of a righteous man speaks of him as one who "does not lend at interest or take any increase." The fundamental difference between the economic order of our world and the economy of ancient Israel is that with us capital is used for the building of productive enterprises which produce profits whereas with the Israelites there was little understanding of the need of capital for economic development. When we consider the fundamental place of capital and credit in industrial progress today, we can realize how far removed we are from the basic assumptions of many of the writers of the Bible.

THE PLACE OF MIRACLES

The difference between the world of the Bible and our world comes to a focus as we seek to deal with the place of miracle in the biblical record. We live in a world in which scientists have increasingly traced the relation between cause and effect in the natural world. We assume the fact that the world of nature is dependable, and we have used this assumption to enable man to understand the laws of his universe and to use the forces of nature for the accomplishment of his purposes.

Of course, we must not permit our knowledge of science to cause us to believe in a closed universe which has no place for the unique action of God. The consistent witness of the New Testament affirms the presence in history of a supernatural person. We cannot make sense of the New Testament if we refuse to accept the witness of the New Testament writers to the mighty works of our Lord. And the efforts of scholars to go behind the Jesus of the

New Testament to a so-called Jesus of history, who would be inoffensive to the modern mind, have failed. In his *The Quest of the Historical Jesus,* Schweitzer shows the inherent contradictions in all of the efforts of German scholarship to discover the "Jesus of history." We must believe that the witness to Jesus which is preserved in the New Testament is in substantial agreement with the facts of his birth, his life, his death, and his resurrection. To deny all of the miraculous element of the New Testament is to destroy the very heart of its message.

In a similar manner we cannot make sense out of the Old Testament unless we believe that there were events in the history of Israel in which the Lord revealed his power in the life of his people. The Old Testament is meaningless without the concept of the Word of the Lord. We must believe that God spoke to the prophets and through the prophets to the life of Israel. The Old Testament cannot be understood as an evolutionary development or progression in which there is no unique action of God. If the Bible is the written record of man's witness to the mighty acts of God, there must be in it something that points to the supernatural.

But when we have fully affirmed our belief in the supernatural both in the New Testament and in the Old, we do have to face the presence in the biblical record of a type of miracle which is perplexing to the modern reader. The ass talks (Numbers 22:28); the sun stands still (Joshua 10:13); the ax swims (2 Kings 6:6); Jonah lives for three days in the belly of the great fish (Jonah 1:17); and the dead come from the tombs to appear to many in the streets of Jerusalem (Matthew 27:53). The problems involved for the modern mind in the presence of this type of miracle center in the way they take place in a setting in which they have little relation to the revelation of God's redemptive power for the salvation of his people. The integrity of the Bible is not tied up with the literal acceptance of every miraculous story that is found in it.

Minor Contradictions

As we consider the human element in the making of the Scriptures, we must face the presence of what seem to be minor contradictions in the biblical record. No competent scholar denies that such contradictions are to be found in the text of the Scripture which we now have. However, there are scholars who claim that these contradictions have been introduced in the transmission of the Scriptures. These scholars would say that these disagreements within the text of Scripture would not have been found in the original manuscripts. To this we can reply that we must deal with the Bible as we have it and not with original manuscripts which are now lost. And our knowledge of the accuracy with which the text of the Scriptures has been established would lead us to feel that some of the problems which confront us in the text we have were present in the original documents. We need to check the first three Gospels with each other. Compare, for example, the story told in Matthew 8:5-13 with the story found in Luke 7:1-10. In the Matthew story the centurion deals with Jesus directly. In the Luke story he sends messengers to Jesus. The message of the story is not affected by this discrepancy in details. But is there any way in which the two stories can be completely harmonized? We need to compare the details of the narrative of the Gospel of John with the story that is told in the first three Gospels. For example, John puts the cleansing of the Temple early in the ministry of Jesus (John 2:13-25). The other evangelists put it after the triumphal entry in the last week of the life of Jesus (Matthew 21:12-17; Mark 11:15-19; Luke 19:45-48). John puts the death of Jesus on the day of preparation for the Passover. The other Gospels seem to indicate that the Last Supper was eaten at the time of the Passover (Matthew 26:2, 17-19; Mark 14:14-16; Luke 22:7, 11, 13, 15). We should examine the accuracy of the quotation of the Old Testament in the letters of Paul.* We can compare the narrative of Kings with that of Chronicles. Compare, for example, the story of the death of Josiah in 2 Kings 23:28-30 with the story in 2 Chronicles 35:20-27. We can study the way Matthew finds the fulfillment of Old Testament prophecy in the first two chapters of his Gospel. The outcome of such a study will make us cautious about insisting upon absolute inerrancy in minor details as necessarily involved in the inspiration of the Scriptures.

* For a detailed discussion of this see Chapter VII in my book *Consider Paul.*

Moral Problems

In the effort to realize the difference between the thought forms of the ancient world and our basic assumptions today, we must remember that in the law of Deuteronomy the worship of false gods by an Israelite is to be punished by death. Consider, for example, Deuteronomy 17:2-7. This passage was used by both Catholics and Protestants to justify the imposing of the death penalty for heresy. We can understand the way the devout Israelites felt about a man who had forsaken the worship of the Lord to follow after false gods. But can we bring the spirit of this passage into harmony with the teachings of Jesus? We fully appreciate the tremendous concept of God which is found in the Old Testament. We find here a God of wrath and justice as well as a God of faithfulness, love, and infinite compassion. But can we bring all the actions attributed to God in the Old Testament into harmony with the God whom Jesus has made known to us?

The Necessity of a Critical Approach

The culminating impact of the human elements in the making of the Scriptures leads us to affirm the necessity for a critical approach to their study. We must ask, of course, that those who would interpret the Scriptures shall stand within the fellowship of the people of God. We must approach the Scriptures reverently, with full willingness to hear their witness to the mighty acts of God. We must approach them in the belief that God has spoken to our fathers through the prophets and that in Jesus Christ the eternal Word has become flesh and dwelt among us. If, however, the Word of God coming to us through the Scriptures is to speak to the need of our age, we must study them with some appreciation of the human elements that have gone into their making. Paul thought of himself as the bearer to both Jew and Gentile of the "light of the knowledge of the glory of God in the face of Christ" (2 Corinthians 4:6). He knew also that he had this treasure in earthen vessels (2 Corinthians 4:7). He was thinking here not so much of the written word as of his own weakness and frailty. He was overcome with the burden of being the mortal bearer of immortal tidings. He goes on to say that the transcendent power which belongs to God is revealed in his capacity to use weak and fallible human beings as the bearer of his message to mankind. We do not do violence to the thought of Paul when we say that the transcendent power of God is revealed in his ability to use the written word as the vehicle of his message to our generation.

THE BIBLE AS INSPIRED OF GOD

We have thought in terms of the human element in the making of the Scripture and with it of the necessity of a reverent critical approach to the study of the Scriptures if we are to hear through them the Word of God. It now becomes necessary to define the sense in which it is proper to say that the Scriptures are inspired of God. We have thought first of revelation event. We have included in the term, revelation event, certain events in history in which God has made himself known and certain experiences in which the Word of God comes to definite individuals in their life situation. The Holy Spirit moves through the revelation events to call into being the people of God, the believing community of the Old or New Testaments. The written word comes into being when those who stand within the fellowship of faith are moved by God to commit to writing their witness to revelation event or their understanding of the message that God would speak through them. The moving of the Spirit of God would be found both in the inspiration of the writers and in the guidance of the church in the selection of these writings to form the canon, the body of writings accepted as authoritative.

We do not have in the New Testament any carefully worked out doctrine of the inspiration of the written word although we do have some suggestions for it. Paul in 1 Corinthians 2:12 is conscious of teaching in words that have come to him under the inspiration of the Holy Spirit. We can be sure that he would be equally conscious of the inspiration of the Holy Spirit when he committed his message to writing in his letters. The inspiration of the Spirit would not mean a guarantee of mechanical inerrancy as he quoted from the Old Testament in his letters, but it would mean that the message of Romans was a true understanding of the meaning of the Christian faith.

The actual statement that the Scriptures are written by men moved by the Holy Spirit is found in 2 Peter 1:21, which reads: "First of all you must understand this, that no prophecy of scripture is a matter of one's own interpretation, because no prophecy ever came by the impulse of man, but *men moved by the Holy Spirit spoke from God."* In their setting these words refer, of course, to the prophets of the Old Testament. But Christians can properly use them to describe the inspiration of the writers of the New Testament.

Paul in his last letter to Timothy says to him: "From childhood you have been acquainted with the sacred writings which are able to instruct you for salvation through faith in Christ Jesus. All scripture is inspired by God and profitable for teaching, for reproof, for correction, and for training in righteousness, that the man of God may be complete, equipped for every good work" (2 Timothy 3:15-17). We should notice here also that Paul is thinking of the Old Testament. But his words deal with the nature of the written Word and can apply to the whole Bible. In these verses Paul definitely says that the Scriptures are inspired of God and that they are able to give the knowledge which is necessary for salvation. He says that this salvation comes not through faith in a Book but through faith in a Person—the Person to whom the Scriptures point. Paul develops this idea in 2 Corinthians 3:12-18 when he tells the Jews that whenever they read Moses they are unable to understand their Scriptures because a veil is over their eyes. He tells them also that if they will turn to the Lord the veil will be taken away. The key to the understanding of the Scriptures of both the Old and the New Testaments is the acknowledgment of Jesus as Lord.

The Authority of the Bible

The authority of the Scriptures is not something that can be established by rational argument. If it could be, the authority could be destroyed if an argument was invalidated. The authority of the Scripture is certainly not to be identified with a doctrine of inerrancy in which the Scriptures cease to be the Word of God if we find in them one proved error in the accuracy of historical details. No man is more profoundly insecure than the man who has tied his sense of the authority of the Bible to the assertion of its inerrancy in every detail. The authority of the Scripture is found in the power of the living Lord to authenticate himself as he speaks to the human heart through the words of the Scripture. The authority of the Scriptures is found in the power of God to speak through them in such a way that they become to the believer an infallible source of faith and life. The authority of the Scriptures is found in the testimony of the Holy Spirit, in the power of the Holy Spirit to testify in our hearts that the message we have received is indeed the Word of God to us. The Westminster Confession of Faith gives expression to this truth when it says of the Scripture: "Our full persuasion and assurance of the infallible truth and divine authority thereof, is from the inward work of the Holy Spirit, bearing witness by and with the word in our hearts" (Chapter I, Section V). We witness to the transcendent power of God when we face frankly the human element in the making of the Scriptures and go on to say that through these writings the living God is able to give an infallible revelation of himself to his people.

QUESTIONS

1. Why is it necessary for the Word of God to come to us in the speech of man?
2. To what extent does this mean that the Word of God which comes to us shares in the frailty of all things human?
3. Why is it necessary for us to seek to establish the correct text of Scripture?
4. Why are the Protestant churches committed to the translation of the Bible into the common speech of every people to which it comes?
5. Suggest some of the thought forms of the Bible which are not familiar to the modern mind.
6. Why is it necessary for us to believe in the supernatural if we are to understand the Bible?
7. Why are some of the miracles of the Bible peculiarly perplexing to the man of today?

8. What are some of the moral problems involved in the interpretation of the Bible?

9. What are some of the contradictions that scholars have found as they have examined the biblical record?

10. Why does the realization of the human element in the making of the Scriptures make necessary a critical approach to the study of the Bible?

11. How does the word of man in the Scriptures become the Word of God?

12. What is your doctrine of the inspiration of the Scriptures?

13. What is the source of the authority of the Bible?

III

Rightly Dividing the Word of Truth

Principles of Biblical Interpretation

THE RECOGNITION of the human element in the making of the Scriptures necessitates, inevitably, a concern for the development of sound principles of biblical interpretation. We must seek to approach the Scripture in such a manner that we receive from it God's Word for our generation. Paul in his last letter to Timothy says: "Do your best to present yourself to God as one approved, a workman who has no need to be ashamed, rightly handling the word of truth" (2 Timothy 2:15). When Paul speaks of the "word of truth" in this verse, he is thinking of the gospel message which has been entrusted to Timothy. Timothy is to seek the approval of God for the fidelity with which he proclaims the word of truth. However, we do not do violence to Paul's message if we apply it to the way we interpret the written word. As we interpret the Scripture, we must be concerned not so much with the praise of men but with the presentation of ourselves to God as workmen who handle the word of truth in a way that is pleasing to him.

As we seek to understand the meaning of Scripture, we must realize that the interpreter of the Scripture should take his stand within the believing community, the church. In the next chapter, we will develop more fully the whole question of involvement as we seek to understand the message of the Bible. We referred at the close of our last chapter to Paul's conviction that the Old Testament could be understood in its deepest meaning only as men interpreted it in the light of its fulfillment in Jesus Christ. We can be certain that the key to understanding the New Testament is the acknowledgment of Jesus Christ as Lord and Saviour. If we reject the central message of the New Testament, the meaning of the book as a whole must be to us an enigma.

The Right of Private Interpretation

Before looking at some principles of interpretation, it is wise to state clearly the Protestant insistence that the Bible should be placed in the hands of the people in their own language. On this point the Westminster Confession of Faith reads: "They [the Scriptures] are to be translated into the language of every people unto which they come, that the word of God dwelling plentifully in all, they may worship him in an acceptable manner, and, through patience and comfort of the Scriptures, may have hope" (Chapter I, Section VIII). When people have the Bible in their own language and can read it for themselves, the Spirit of God can speak through it to their need.

We must not overestimate the difficulty of understanding the Bible. The Bible is not a book for scholars alone. It is a book which even the man whose education has been limited can read and understand. The Westminster Confession of Faith says: "All things in Scripture are not alike plain in themselves, nor alike clear unto all; yet those things which are necessary to be known, believed, and observed, for salvation, are so clearly propounded and opened in some place of Scripture or other, that not only the learned, but the unlearned, in a due use of the ordinary means, may attain unto a sufficient understanding of them" (Chapter I, Section VII).

The right of private interpretation of the Scriptures is a sacred right in Protestantism. The church cannot keep the Scriptures from the people, and the church cannot arrogate to itself the authority to tell the people what the Scriptures mean. The depth of understanding that is often found in those who have had very little training in how to study the Bible is amazing. But the man who insists on his right to interpret the Bible for himself does have the responsibility of seeking, as far as he can, to understand

and use sound principles of biblical interpretation. In this chapter, we will attempt to set forth a number of principles of interpretation by which a reader may come to an understanding of the Bible's message.

WHAT DOES IT SAY?

The first and most important principle in the study of the Scriptures is the discipline by which we attempt to find what a passage really says. This may not be as simple as it would seem at first thought. There is a frequently told story which illustrates this. A professor of biology left a specimen of fish with a student and told him to look at it. At first the student glanced at the specimen and felt that there was little more he could do. He had seen it and he was through. At the insistence of the professor, however, he went back to the fish for more observation. Then he realized that he had not really seen it at all. Finally he scrutinized that one specimen of fish for many hours. As a result, he came out of the study of this one fish with lessons in the observation of a specimen which were invaluable to him as he continued his study in biology.*

A similar process can take place in the study of a passage of Scripture. At first we read it over and we think we have finished our task. Then we realize that we have not come to grips with what the passage means. Our first task is to determine what the man who wrote it meant to say to the people to whom it was originally written. To do this we will need to see the passage in its context. Very often people read into a verse a meaning which the words of the verse will carry, but it may be obvious when the verse is seen in context that the meaning given it does not fit the setting. A typical example of this is Romans 14:7 which reads: "None of us lives to himself, and none of us dies to himself." The language of this verse beautifully expresses the idea that every man lives in some measure in a responsible relation to other people. This is a true idea, but it is not the idea which Paul expressed in the

* This story under the title "The Student, the Fish and Agassiz" is found in *Appendix American Problems,* Houghtons, Osgood & Co., 1880.

verse. As the next verse clearly shows, Paul is saying that every man both in life and death is responsible to the Lord.

If we are to know what a passage really says, we may need to study carefully the meaning which the writer puts into the key words of the passage. For this we may need the help of dictionaries and commentaries. Very often, however, all we need is just to look at the passage long enough and hard enough to quit reading into it what we want it to say and to hear, perhaps for the first time, what the writer is really trying to tell his readers. In this kind of discipline a knowledge of the original languages is helpful, but it is certainly not always essential. We may find it wise to read the key verses in different translations. By comparing translations we can often understand what different scholars thought the original language meant. We may want to compare our understanding of what the passage means with interpretations that are given in recommended commentaries. But the first rule of Bible study is to use the tools at our disposal to come to an understanding of what the passage we are considering means. It is only after we have exhausted our own resources that we should turn to the help of others.

Literal and Figurative

A second principle of interpretation is that we must distinguish between figurative language and language which is meant to be taken literally. Consider from this point of view Matthew 5:27-30. Jesus in this passage is discussing the struggle for purity. He is saying that no price is too heavy to pay for the achievement of purity. He does not mean that we should mutilate ourselves; we will not gain purity by plucking out an eye or cutting off a hand; yet we must be ready to put ruthlessly out of our life anything that leads to impurity of thought or life.

Permanent and Universal or Local and Temporary

We must be able to distinguish between the things in the Bible which are local and temporary and those that are permanent and universal. Paul's instructions that women should be veiled when praying may have been wise in the situation he faced (1 Corinthians 11:5-7), but this does not mean that women are permanently obligated to wear their hats in church. The prohibition of the taking of interest which we considered in our last chapter may have made sense in Hebrew society. It would not be wise to insist upon it as a necessary characteristic of Christian character today. Paul advised the Corinthians against marriage "in view of the impending distress," (1 Corinthians 7:26). This does not mean that his advice should be binding in a different situation.

FROM WORDS TO IDEAS

We must go behind the words of Scripture to the great ideas which the writers are seeking to express. A study of the letter to the Hebrews will illustrate this. The writer of this letter uses expressions and processes of reasoning that were accepted in the circles in which he moved. At first we may find him hard to follow, and we may feel that his line of argument is not very convincing. When we begin to grasp his ideas, such as the finality of Christianity, the work of Jesus as high priest, and the meaning of faith, we find, however, that this letter is tremendously relevant to the needs of the modern world. The way to remain permanently fresh in our teaching is to study the Scriptures until we have gone behind the words and understood the ideas of its writers so clearly that we are able to communicate them to others.

THE WITNESS TO REVELATION EVENT

The Bible is a written record in which men of faith have endeavored to preserve for us their understanding of events through which God has made himself known to his people. It is therefore a sound principle of biblical interpretation for us to seek to discover the events to which the biblical writers would direct our attention and the understanding of the significance of these events which the writers of the Scriptures would communicate to us. As we read the story of the Exodus, we must realize that it is to these events that the Hebrews looked for their knowledge of the way their God had delivered them. When we read the narrative of the fall of Jerusalem, we must not forget that Jeremiah saw in this event the encounter of Israel with her God.

After John has told the story of the first miracle of Jesus at Cana of Galilee, he gives its significance as he writes: "This, the first of his signs, Jesus did at Cana in Galilee, and *manifested his glory; and his disciples believed on him* (John 2:11). In a similar manner Jesus gives the significance of the raising of Lazarus in his prayer that through this miracle those who are standing by may know that the Father has sent him (John 11:42). When Luke has told the story of the death of Jesus, he tells also of the appearance of the risen Lord in which he explains to Cleopas and his companion that it was necessary for the Christ to suffer these things and to enter into his glory (Luke 24:26).

Seeking the Central Message

As we interpret Scripture, we must seek the central message of a story and not permit ourselves to become unduly absorbed with the marginal. The heart of the story of David's anointing (1 Samuel 16:1-13) is found in the words: "The Lord sees not as man sees; man looks on the outward appearance, but the Lord looks on the heart." In the account of the rejection of Saul which precedes this story (1 Samuel 15:1-34), we face the problem of understanding the war against Amalek as an expression of God's will for Israel. We must not, however, allow our absorption with this problem to prevent us from seeing that the heart of the story is the test of Saul's obedience as the Anointed of the Lord to the Word of the Lord which he has received through Samuel. When Samuel says to Saul: "Behold, to obey is better than sacrifice, and to hearken than the fat of rams," he is giving a prophetic insight into the nature of God's demands upon his people.

In our study of the parables of Jesus, we should remember that the crucial thing is to get the central thrust of the parable. We will miss the meaning of a parable if we feel that some special significance has to be found for each of the details. Jesus himself does not hesitate to liken God to an unjust judge or to illustrate the wisdom of laying up treasures in heaven by the example of an unrighteous steward. This does not mean that he teaches that God is unjust or that he approves of the conduct of the steward. His concern is that we should learn from one parable the importance of persistence in prayer and from the other the wisdom of using the time that we have left in the life on earth to prepare for the life of heaven (Luke 18:1-8 and Luke 16:1-9).

SEEKING THE ABIDING HUMAN SITUATION

As we deal with the biblical narrative, we must seek the abiding human situation in the encounter of man with God. Human life in the last few generations has changed amazingly in its material aspects. Yet when we think in terms of sin and forgiveness and man's need of God, we find that we have much in common with the men and women of the Bible. There is something eternally significant in the story in which Nathan confronts David in his sin (2 Samuel 12:1-23) or the picture of Elijah waiting for Ahab in Naboth's vineyard (1 Kings 21:1-29). The request of Philip, "Lord, show us the Father" (John 14:8), can be our word to Jesus and Jesus' answer to him can become his answer to us. The Bible can become the place of our encounter with God.

INTERPRETING SCRIPTURE BY SCRIPTURE

"The infallible rule of interpretation of Scripture, is the Scripture itself; and therefore, when there is a question about the true and full sense of any scripture (which is not manifold, but one), it may be searched and known by other places that speak more clearly." (Westminster Confession of Faith, Chapter I, Section IX). It is a sound principle of biblical interpretation that we seek to understand difficult or obscure passages of the Scripture in the light of passages in which the meaning is clear. In doing this we do not impose an artificial unity upon the Scripture. The task of biblical interpretation is to seek to understand clearly the meaning of a passage of Scripture without being too much concerned whether the message of this passage is in agreement with the meaning of other passages. There is, however, a deep unity to the Scripture as a whole. This unity arises from the fact that the writers of Scripture share a common understanding of the meaning of the revelation of God in Christ. The church has included in its canon of Scripture only those writings which are in harmony with the central meaning of its faith. The person who seeks to understand the meaning of a particular passage of Scripture should seek to interpret it in the light of the Bible's message as a whole. Underlying the variety of form and expression which we have in the Scriptures is a deep unity which comes from the fact that the various writers have been moved by *one Spirit.*

If we are studying the witness to the virgin birth which is found in Matthew and Luke, it is proper to supplement this by the witness to the pre-existence of the Christ which is found in the writings of John and Paul (Matthew 1:18-24; Luke 1:26-38; John 1:1-17; Philippians 2:6-8). If we are studying the concise statement of the implications of Christian faith for Christian living found in 1 Thessalonians 5:12-22, we will need to interpret the things that are said here in the light of a fuller statement found in Romans 12:9-21. If we are studying what Paul says about marriage in the seventh chapter of 1 Corinthians, we need to compare what he said to the Corinthians with what he said about those who "forbid marriage" in 1 Timothy 4:1-4. If we are dealing with the doctrine of the death of Christ as an atonement for sin set forth by Paul in Romans 5:6-11, we should also study 1 John 4:10. It is by comparing Scripture with Scripture that we gain our best insights into the full meaning of our faith. "The infallible rule of the interpretation of Scripture, is the Scripture itself" (Westminster Confession of Faith, Chapter I, Section IX).

In Accordance with the Tradition

Another sound rule for the interpretation of the Scripture is to seek to learn through the better commentaries how a passage has been understood by the expositors of Scripture through the ages. We do not need to be bound by these expositions, but before we go our independent way we should know what other men have said concerning the meaning of a passage and why they have said it. When we study the great interpreters of the Bible, we will find that every reader brings to the Bible certain presuppositions which inevitably affect what he finds in the Scripture. We would hope that our presuppositions have been formed by the Scriptures and that we would be constantly ready to revise them as the Spirit speaks to us through the Scriptures. But the point of view from which we approach the Scriptures does affect the way in which we hear their message.

For example, when a Roman Catholic scholar comes upon the references to the brothers and sisters of Jesus in Matthew 13:55-56, he is certain to insist that they are either children of Joseph by a former marriage or cousins of Jesus. His interpretation will not be based on anything that he finds in the Scripture but on the Roman Catholic insistence on the perpetual virginity of Mary. When a scholar who believes in apostolic succession as the mark of a true church reads the references to the laying on of hands in the letters to Timothy, he is certain to find in them a depth of meaning which a scholar who stands in the Presbyterian and Reformed tradition will not discover. A Presbyterian will be sure that the government of the church by elders is involved in the way Paul organized his churches. We should be willing to let the Bible speak for itself even if it means rethinking our basic assumptions, but it is better for an interpreter of the Bible to stand in a tradition that has been tested through the ages than for him to approach the Bible in ignorance of all that has been said and done by the devout scholars of the past to help us understand the Bible.

THE RELEVANCE OF THE BIBLE TO LIFE

We have been thinking of the discipline through which we endeavor to understand the true message of the Scripture. We have sought to know what the original writer meant to say to his readers. Yet we have never adequately dealt with the divine truth of the Scriptures until we have sought to see the meaning of this truth for us. The Word of God which came to men in the Old Testament was usually a word of command to a man or to a people. It was a message from God which called for decision. It was a message which men must hear or fail to hear at their peril. The Christ who today speaks to us from the Scriptures calls us to decision and action. When we have heard the Word of the Lord which was spoken in the *there* and the *then,* we must ask its meaning for us in the *here* and the *now.* As we shall see in the study of involvement in the next chapter, our very capacity to hear the Word of God is related to our willingness to be obedient to it.

It is crucial for the reader of the Bible to realize that it contains a message which is pertinent to him. A man may read the Bible because he is interested in the stories it tells. It is a great book of stories. He may continue to read because he enjoys the majesty of its style or the beauty of its poetry. But if a man is to understand the Bible, he must soon come to know that this Book is saying something to him which concerns him deeply. He must come to realize that his deepest satisfactions in this life and the salvation of his immortal soul are related to the reaction which he himself makes to the message of this Book.

The message of the Bible is seldom to the individual alone. If we have studied the Bible until its great ideas have emerged and laid hold upon us, we will find that we are forced to look at the whole life of man in the light of the truth which has come from God. If we have studied deeply the meaning of the Bible, we will find that its great ideas confront us in the context of our earthly life and call in question many of the accepted customs of our society. The Word of the Lord can come to us as a word of assurance and hope. It can come also as a word of offense that has revolutionary implications for our society. The God who makes himself known to us in the Bible is a God who requires us "to do justice." He is a God who is eternally hostile to evil. He is a God who shows no partiality in his dealings with men. The Christ to whom the Scriptures bear witness can become the Great Disturber of our society's complacency. There is no greater heresy than that of toning down our Christian teaching until the message which we proclaim from the Scriptures has no relevancy to the crucial issues of our contemporary society.

Jesus as Lord of the Scripture

A final principle of interpretation of the Scriptures is the recognition that the Scripture itself must be judged by its agreement with the Lord Jesus Christ. Jesus knew that he came as the consummation of the revelation of God which is found in the Old Testament. He said to his contemporaries: "Think not that I have come to abolish the law and the prophets; I have not come to abolish them but to fulfil them" (Matthew 5:17). On many occasions Jesus insisted that his mission was the true development of the movement of the Old Testament. In the Gospel of John, Jesus appeals to the Scriptures in his debates with the Jews. He says to those who have refused to believe on him: "You search the scriptures, because you think that in them you have eternal life; and it is they that bear witness to me" (John 5:39). He closes this discourse by saying to his adversaries: "If you believed Moses, you would believe me, for he wrote of me. But if you do not believe his writings, how will you believe my words?" (John 5:46-47.) In the closing chapter of Luke's Gospel the risen Lord says to Cleopas and his friend: "O foolish men, and slow of heart to believe all that the prophets have spoken!" (Luke 24:25.) And Luke tells us that "beginning with Moses and all the prophets, he interpreted to them in all the scriptures the things concerning himself" (Luke 24:27). Luke tells us also that in the first appearance of the risen Lord to the eleven "he opened their minds to understand the scriptures" (Luke 24:45).

The Jesus who insisted that he did not come to abolish the law and the prophets but to fulfill them could say also to the men of his generation: "Ye have heard that it was said to the men of old . . . But I say to you" (Matthew 5:21-22, K.J.V.). In the teachings of Jesus there is a contrast between the old and the new which cannot be denied. Jesus proceeds to deepen men's understanding of the sixth and seventh commandments. He repudiates the law of divorce as given by Moses (Deuteronomy 24:1-4) and reaffirms the finality of marriage. He substitutes for the law of revenge as found in the Old Testament (Exodus 21:24; Leviticus 24:20; Deuteronomy 19:21) the principle of nonresistance to evil and the command to turn the other cheek. He expands the command to love your neighbor as yourself as found in Leviticus 19:18 to include also the love of enemies. The way of life which Jesus sets forth goes beyond the ethics of the Old Testament. The followers of Jesus found their final revelation of God in the one whom they knew to be God manifest in the flesh. They believed that the ultimate truth concerning God had been revealed to them in

Jesus. The concept of God in the Old Testament has to be judged in the light of the knowledge of the glory of God as seen in Jesus Christ. The norm by which Scripture itself is to be judged is the mind and heart of the Lord Jesus Christ as he is witnessed to in the New Testament.

QUESTIONS

These questions are intended to involve the reader who wishes to work through them in the principles of biblical interpretation that have been set forth in this chapter.

1. Read Jeremiah 6:14 and 8:11. How does the setting of these verses help you to understand the sin of the prophets who were crying peace! peace! when there was no peace?

2. Read Luke 14:26. What do you understand Jesus to mean when he says that anyone who comes after him must hate his own father and mother?

3. Read Jesus' directions to the seventy in Luke 10:1-12. Notice especially Luke 10:4. Compare this passage with Luke 22:35-38. What are some of the directions of Jesus to the seventy that may be local and temporary in their application?

4. Read 1 Thessalonians 1:1-8. What did Paul mean when he told the Thessalonians that the will of God for them was their *sanctification?* How does the context help you to understand the meaning of the word sanctification in this passage?

5. Read 1 Corinthians 9:1-2. What is the event to which Paul refers when he asks the question: "Have I not seen Jesus our Lord?" What is the significance of his reference to this event in this setting?

6. Read Luke 15:1-2. What is the setting in which Jesus tells the three parables in the fifteenth chapter of Luke? How does the knowledge of this setting help us to understand the central message in each of these parables?

7. Read 2 Samuel 18:24-33. What is there that is timeless in the conflict in the soul of David as his army goes out to battle with Absalom and his followers? What is the relation between the sin of David and the death of Absalom? See 2 Samuel 12:10. How does this help us to see the judgment of God in the life of David?

8. Read Philippians 2:5-7. Compare these verses with Galatians 4:4. Do these passages support the belief in the pre-existence of Jesus? Compare them with John 1:1-4, 14 and 8:58.

9. Read Mark 7:1-13. What does Jesus have to say here about the dangers involved in the traditions of the elders? How had these traditions been used to avoid the obligations involved in the sixth commandment?

10. Read Matthew 7:21-28. What does Jesus say here about the necessity of translating into deeds the teachings we have received from him?

11. Read Matthew 5:21-48. How often does Jesus in these verses use the formula: "It was said . . . but I say." How does this passage assert the claim of Jesus to be the Lord of the Scripture?

IV

Obedience — the Road to Spiritual Knowledge

The Necessity of Involvement

AS WE HAVE CONSIDERED the principles of biblical interpretation, we have been forced at various places to realize the necessity of personal involvement if we are to understand the Bible. The message we receive from the Bible is related to the way we respond to it. There are spiritual conditions for the apprehension of spiritual truth. We have thought of the insights of the Bible in terms of their relevance to life. Yet our capacity to hear the Bible's message as it pertains to the crucial issues of our time is affected by our willingness to seek to be obedient to the insights of biblical faith when we have received them. To some men the message of the gospel can be the key to the understanding of the deepest mysteries of human existence. To other men the same message can be folly and offense. The difference is to be found in their willingness to respond or in their refusal to hear the proclamation of the Word of God. It is our purpose in this chapter to examine the necessity of personal response to the message of the Bible and its implications both for faith and unbelief.

Hearing and Obeying the Word in the Old Testament

The necessity of response to God's revelation of himself is apparent throughout the biblical story. Whenever God has spoken to man, his Word has demanded a response from man. This is as true in the Old Testament as it is in the New. The

Christian teacher, therefore, can never be content simply to repeat to his class what the biblical writers said centuries ago. He must seek always to help his pupils hear and respond to what God is telling them through the Scripture. The pupil must be actively involved in a dynamic encounter, learning and obeying God's personal message to him, or he really does not understand the Bible at all.

The Word of the Lord which came to the men of the Old Testament never came simply as a word of information revealing abstract principles about the character of God and the nature of his will for man. It came always as a word of command. It involved, on the part of those who received it, an element of decision which led either to obedience or disobedience.

The Call of Abraham. The word that comes to Abraham is a word that is to be heard and obeyed. The writer of Genesis tells us that the Lord said to Abraham: "Go from your country and your kindred and your father's house to the land that I will show you" (Genesis 12:1). The promise of the blessing which Abraham was to receive was conditional upon his obedience to the divine command. Abraham "went out, not knowing where he was to go" (Hebrews 11:8). We have here the beginning of a spiritual pilgrimage in which Abraham, over a period of many years, is tested until he reveals that his readiness to be obedient to the Word of the Lord takes precedence even over his love for Isaac, the heir of the promises. Abraham's belief in the power of the Lord to keep promises and his own readiness to obey the Word of the Lord makes him the spiritual father of all those who respond to the Word of the Lord in faith and in obedience. The faith of Abraham is never something for the reader of the Scripture to contemplate without personal involvement. Jesus tells the leaders of the Jews that if they are to be the spiritual children of Abraham they must do the works of Abraham, i.e., respond in faith to the Word of God which they have received through him (John 8:39-40). Paul finds the true children of Abraham in those who believe in the God who raised the Lord Jesus from the dead (Romans 4:24). We are the children of Abraham today when we respond in faith and obedience to the call of God which comes through Jesus Christ. If our study of the Bible does not lead to such response, it is incomplete.

His Ways to Moses. When God makes himself known to Moses at Horeb, he speaks to him in a way which calls for belief and obedience. Moses is called to become the deliverer of his people from their bondage to the Egyptians. As he goes to Egypt in obedience to the Lord's command, he is given an understanding of the nature of God and of the will of God for man which makes him the real founder of the faith of Israel.

His Acts to the Children of Israel. In the history of Israel as a whole there is always the understanding of the life of faith as a spiritual pilgrimage in which the people are called upon to be obedient to God's commands. The religion of the Hebrews was intensely practical. It involved a knowledge of God which had been transmitted through the great events of their history. With this knowledge of God, however, there was always the obligation to serve the Lord with fidelity. The great mystery of the Old Testament is the ease with which the Hebrews failed to remember the mighty acts of their God and neglected their responsibilities as his covenant people. We think of the wilderness experience as the time when the Lord made himself known in a peculiar way to his people. Yet those who told the history of Israel were amazed at the capacity of the people to rebel against the commandments of their God. Beginning with the worship of the golden calf in the shadow of Sinai, we have repeated examples of the failure of the Israelites to be obedient to the Word of the Lord that had been revealed to them through Moses. It was a failure which meant that the generation that left Egypt did not enter Canaan. When the actual conquest of the land under Joshua's leadership had been accomplished a generation later, the children of Israel entered upon a long period of history in which they alternated between remembering the Lord and serving him and forgetting the Lord and giving their allegiance to false gods.

The Word of the Lord to Isaiah. During the latter part of the history of the Hebrew nation, there appeared a number of great prophets who were the bearers of a Word of God to their generation. Much of their message has been preserved for us in writing. Among the greatest of the prophets was Isaiah. He is typical of all of those who received the Word of the Lord in the Old Testament because the call to him demands his personal response. In the scene which is described for us in the sixth chapter of Isaiah, we have Isaiah's vision of the holiness of God, his sense of forgiveness, and his consciousness of the removal of guilt. The call comes to Isaiah as he hears the voice of the Lord saying: "Whom shall I send, and who will go for us?" He responds to the call: "Here I am! Send me." It is at this time that Isaiah receives a message that shocks us. He is told that the consequences of his preaching in the lives of many of his contemporaries will be a process of hardening; they will reject his word and become increasingly insensitive to spiritual things. The Lord says to him:

> Go and say to this people:
> "Hear and hear, but do not understand;
> see and see, but do not perceive."
> Make the heart of this people fat,
> and their ears heavy,
> and shut their eyes;
> lest they see with their eyes,
> and hear with their ears,
> and understand with their hearts,
> and turn and be healed.
>
> (Isaiah 6:9-10.)

These verses warn us of the consequences of our personal reaction to the Word of the Lord. There is a terrible danger connected with the study of the Bible. If we receive the Word and heed it, the coming of the message of God to us may be the means of repentance and healing. If, however, we refuse to hear the Word of God, our contact with it may be the occasion of our moving forward in a process of hardening. If we hearken to the Word of the Lord, we receive the insights necessary for the understanding of our human existence. On the other hand, if we harden our hearts and refuse to listen, we lose our capacity to hear the message that could have been our salvation. If we are shocked at the forceful way this truth is stated in Isaiah, we will probably be surprised to learn that the verses we are considering are referred to frequently in the New Testament. The New Testament writers turn to them often because the words which were originally spoken to Isaiah express for the New Testament evangelists their own sense of mystery and wonder as they contemplate the unbelief of their contemporaries. Jesus quotes these verses to explain the necessity for presenting his teaching in a veiled form in parables (Matthew 13:14-15; Mark 4:12; Luke 8:10). John expresses through the words spoken of Isaiah his own amazement at the unbelief of the contemporaries of Jesus (John 12:39-41). Paul quotes the same verses in his final encounter with the Jews in Rome (Acts 28:26-27). He refers to them again in his letter to the Romans as he seeks in the eleventh chapter to wrestle with the unbelief of Israel (Romans 11:7-8).

The message which was given to Isaiah becomes a word of warning to the men of every generation including our own. "God sent the Son into the world, not to condemn the world, but that the world might be saved through him" (John 3:17). Jesus concludes one of his debates with the Pharisees by saying: "For judgment I came into this world, that those who do not see may see, and that those who see may become blind" (John 9:39). Every call to faith in which the living Lord confronts us, including every time we study the Bible, may become to those who receive it either a time of salvation or a day of judgment.

Revelation and Response in the First Three Gospels

The principle of personal response as the road to the understanding of the message of God which we have seen in the Old Testament is characteristic of the movement of the first three Gospels. The followers of Jesus are never to be thought of as detached spectators. They are always followers of the way. According to Mark, Jesus begins his ministry preaching the gospel of God and saying, "The time is fulfilled, and the kingdom of God is at hand; repent, and believe the gospel" (Mark 1:15). In the beginning, the message of Jesus includes a call to repentance and faith. As he calls Simon and Andrew to become his disciples, he says to them: "Follow me and I will make you become fishers of men." The promise that he will make them fishers of men is conditioned upon their readiness to follow him.

In Matthew 11:25-30, we have a remarkable passage in which Jesus speaks in a language similar to that of the Gospel of John. (The passage with the exception of the great invitation at its close is repeated in Luke 10:21-22.) In these verses Jesus says that in the providence of God the deepest mysteries of life have been hidden from the wise and prudent. He goes on to say that they are now being revealed to his disciples. He then makes the tremendous affirmation that "no one knows the Father except the Son and any one to whom the Son chooses to reveal him" (Matthew 11:27). This is a profound statement of the nature of spiritual truth. The knowledge of God which Jesus has given man is not something that men can receive without being personally involved in their reactions to it. Jesus follows the statement that he alone has the power to reveal the Father with the great invitation which is addressed to all who labor and are heavy laden. Here also there is a spiritual condition to the rest which Jesus offers. He promises to give his rest to those who will take his yoke upon them and learn from him. He reminds those who seek for his rest that he is meek and lowly in heart. The knowledge of God which Jesus has come to give is not for the proud and haughty.

In the scene at Caesarea Philippi, Jesus tells Peter that the capacity to recognize him as the Christ, the Son of the living God, has been given to him, Peter, by the Father in heaven (Matthew 16:15). In the invitation to discipleship which follows this discourse Jesus says to his disciples: "If any man would come after me, let him deny himself and take up his cross and follow me. For whoever would save his life will lose it, and whoever loses his life for my sake will find it." There is no such thing as a discipleship of Jesus which does not include personal involvement. The great truths of the gospel have to be lived into. They are not abstract statements of truth which men can grasp without any sense of personal commitment.

OBEDIENCE, THE ROAD TO SPIRITUAL KNOWLEDGE

We have discussed the necessity of personal involvement for understanding the Bible as this concept is set forth in the Old Testament and in the first three Gospels. Now we can look at the

Gospel of John and the letters of Paul, particularly the letters to the Corinthians. It is here that we have our clearest statements of the spiritual conditions necessary for apprehending today the truths that have been made known through revelation. In his prologue, John gives his understanding of who Jesus was—the pre-existent Word of God, who is himself God. He writes: "In the beginning was the Word, and the Word was with God, and the Word was God" (John 1:1). In the fourteenth verse, John continues: "And the Word became flesh and dwelt among us, full of grace and truth; we have beheld his glory, glory as of the only Son from the Father." It is with this exalted view of the person of Jesus that John sets forth the consequences of our response to him. He writes: "He [Jesus] came to his own home, and his own people received him not. But to all who received him, who believed in his name, he gave power to become children of God, who were born, not of blood nor of the will of the flesh nor of the will of man, but of God" (John 1:11-13).

This doctrine of the new birth, which is stated in general terms in the prologue, is illustrated in the story of Nicodemus. Nicodemus comes to Jesus from his background as a Pharisee, a member of the Sanhedrin, and a recognized teacher of Israel. He and his friends have reached the conviction that Jesus is a teacher sent from God. They have come to this conviction because they are sure than no man can do the signs which Jesus has done unless God is with him. But Nicodemus comes by night. He does not wish to be seen talking with the teacher from Nazareth. Nicodemus has no intention of sacrificing his position as a teacher of Israel by becoming a follower of the Nazarene. He does, however, want to talk with Jesus. He comes to Jesus as the detached observer who would like to ask some questions. He wants to talk to Jesus, but he does not seek personal involvement.

Jesus tells Nicodemus that he cannot stop with casual conversation about the Christ. He insists that Nicodemus must be born anew if he is to see the Kingdom of God. He spells out his meaning when he says to Nicodemus: "Truly, truly, I say to you, unless one is born of water and the Spirit, he cannot enter the kingdom of God." Jesus asks of Nicodemus two things. The first is an act of inner surrender which will allow the Spirit of God to work in him the miracle of the new birth. "Born of water" is probably a reference to baptism as the sign of public identification with Jesus. If this understanding of the text is correct, Jesus asks Nicodemus as the second thing to follow the act of inner surrender with a public profession of faith in Jesus. Nicodemus is not ready for meeting either of these conditions when he comes to Jesus: He has come in the night and he goes in the night. He may be the teacher of Israel, but he cannot enter the Kingdom of God apart from personal commitment. The modern Bible teacher must take note.

The principle which is illustrated in the story of Nicodemus is repeated again and again in the Gospel of John. We find it in John 7:16-17. In his debate with the Jews, Jesus says: "My teaching is not mine, but his who sent me; if any man's will is to do his will, he shall know whether the teaching is from God or whether I am speaking on my own authority." In these verses, obedience is clearly set forth as the road to spiritual knowledge. If any man is genuinely willing to do the will of God, there will be given to him the certainty that the teaching of Jesus is from God.

The same idea is set forth in John 8:12 under the figure of light and darkness. Jesus says: "I am the light of the world; he who follows me will not walk in darkness, but will have the light of life." The condition for receiving the light of life is the readiness to follow Jesus.

WISDOM AND POWER OR FOLLY AND OFFENSE

In his practical experience as a Christian evangelist in Corinth, Paul faces the necessity of involvement if we are to receive the message of the gospel. In Corinth, as in other cities, Paul gave his witness to the resurrection and his burning message that God through the death of Christ was reconciling the world unto himself. He found that many of the Greeks branded his message as "foolishness." They had no place in their philosophy for the story of the Resurrection. They did not intend to be saved by putting their faith in a crucified Jew. Many of the Jews in Corinth found his message equally unacceptable. They had no room in their thinking for a suffering and dying Messiah. Paul knew, however, that through his preaching there had been called into being a community of believers in Corinth. They were made up of both Jews and Greeks. To those who had received the message, Jesus Christ had become the power of God and the wisdom of God. As the wisdom of God, Christ had enabled them to see the life of man in the light of God. As the power of God, he had given them the capacity to live as children of God.

In reflecting on this fact, Paul asserts the necessity of personal involvement if we are to hear the Word of God. He says that the world has not known God through wisdom. He has stood in Athens, the center of Greek intellectual life, and his spirit has been moved within him as he has seen the city given to idolatry. Paul is convinced that it is part of the wisdom of God that man should not find God through wisdom. God has closed the door to human wisdom as a means of finding ultimate reality so that men might be willing to hear the revelation which has been given in Jesus Christ. It is in this setting that Paul writes: "The unspiritual man does not receive the gifts of the Spirit of God, for they are folly to him, and he is not able to understand them because they are spiritually discerned" (1 Corinthians 2:14).

Paul is certain that the initial acknowledgment of Jesus as Lord is the work of the Holy Spirit. He writes to the Corinthians: "I want you to understand that . . . no one can say 'Jesus is Lord' except by the Holy Spirit" (1 Corinthians 12:3). He is equally certain that there is given to those who have committed themselves to follow Jesus an assured knowledge of a great body of truth which is meaningless to the unconverted. He writes:

> "What no eye has seen, nor ear heard,
> nor the heart of man conceived,
> what God has prepared for those who love him,"
> God has revealed to us through the Spirit.
> (1 Corinthians 2:9-10.)

These words have been used to picture the hope of Heaven, but Paul is using them to describe the truth that has already been revealed through the Spirit to the children of God here on earth.

We must not use this understanding of the message of the gospel as foolishness and offense to the unbeliever and wisdom and power to the believer to deny the absolute nature of truth. Truth does not cease to be the truth simply because I am unaware of it or refuse to believe it. There is a world of objective reality which we may dimly apprehend. Yet its existence is not dependent upon our ideas concerning it. If at the heart of the universe there is a God of love, this God exists independently of what an individual thinks of him. But no truth has power to transform life until it is believed. The church is not the source of truth, but the church is the community that God has called into being to witness to the truth.

THE WAY OF UNBELIEF AND THE WAY OF FAITH

Having scanned the Bible story for its teaching on the necessity of involvement, let us think now of the importance of personal response on the part of a Bible reader today. Let us think together of a man who sets out to read and study the Bible. Let us assume that up to this time he has had little or no serious contact with the Bible or with the Christian faith. At first this man will read the Bible as he might read any other great book. He will seek to understand its meaning in the context in which it was written. Very soon, however, he will begin to realize that the writers of the Bible point always beyond themselves to God. As the reader moves into the New Testament, he will find that the New Testament as a whole points to the coming of God in Christ. It might be possible for such a man to study the Bible with a high degree of empathy. A great scholar could give a sympathetic account of Egyptian religion without finding himself personally committed to any of the ideas which were dominant in that faith. But if a man continued to read the Bible and meditate on its meaning, he would find himself being brought inevitably to the point of decision. He would realize that he had to decide whether or not he believed in the actual existence of the God to whom the Bible points. And as our reader saturated himself with the New Testament message, he would have to decide whether or not he believed that Jesus Christ was in truth the Son of God.

If our reader decided not to yield himself in faith and obedience to the God to whom the Scriptures point, he would find that he was forced to move almost inevitably into some of the attitudes characteristic of unbelief. If he began his studies as a professed atheist, he would need to account for the tremendous God-consciousness which pervades the whole of the Bible. If he rejected the New Testament understanding of Jesus as God manifest in the flesh, he would find that he had to explain in some manner the appearance of the believing community found in the New Testament. In time, he would be led to enigma, to the effort to explain something that cannot be explained within the premises of a secular philosophy. And if our reader reacted violently to the imperious nature of the claims of Jesus, he would be led to offense. The proper opposite of faith is offense.

If, however, our reader came to the place of acknowledging Jesus Christ as Saviour and Lord, he would find that in this acknowledgment he had the key to the understanding of the Scriptures. He would then begin to discover meaning and value in passages which up to this time had been meaningless. If he took seriously the commitment of his life to Jesus Christ, he would find himself compelled to witness to others concerning that which God had done for him in Christ. As he sought to do this, he would find himself turning to the experiences of the men and women of the Bible for guidance in his spiritual pilgrimage. He would read with fresh appreciation the letters of Paul to the first-century Christian communities.

If our original reader finally gave himself without reserve to the service of God in Christ, he would find that through the study of the Bible he was entering upon a whole new world of spiritual reality. He would discover in the Bible the insights to guide him in his earthly pilgrimage, and he would find in it the hope of an eternal redemption.

Questions

1. Why is it that the great truths set forth in the Bible cannot be apprehended apart from commitment of life?

2. How does the story of Abraham involve the reader of the Bible in the necessity of decision?

3. Read Hebrews 11:23-28. What does the writer of Hebrews find in the story of Moses that will be meaningful to his readers?

4. Read Isaiah 6:1-13. How does the experience of Isaiah involve you in your response to God? Why are the ninth and tenth verses of the sixth chapter of Isaiah quoted so frequently in the New Testament? Can you think of any personal experiences in which you could express your reaction through these verses?

5. What are the conditions of discipleship which Jesus sets forth in the first three Gospels? How are the promises of the Christ related to obedience to his commands?

6. Trace the development of faith and the hardening of unbelief in the Gospel of John.

7. Is it proper in your opinion to understand Nicodemus as an example of the detached spectator? How does he illustrate the necessity of the New Birth?

8. What does Jesus mean when he says that he is the light of the world? What is the condition that we must meet if we are not to walk in darkness?

9. How can the preaching of Christ crucified be to some people "folly" and "offense" and to others "wisdom" and "power"?

10. What do we mean when we speak of the "objective reality of truth"?

11. Why is it necessary for an idea to be believed before it can have power to mold our lives?

12. How does unbelief lead to enigma and offense?

13. How does the acknowledgment of God in Christ lead to a deepening understanding of the message of the Bible?

 V

Living by the Word of God

The Life of Man in the Light of God

IN THE LAST CHAPTER, we faced the fact that one must become involved if he is to apprehend spiritual truth. We saw that the preaching of Christ crucified could mean to some men folly and offense and to others wisdom and power. It is possible for two people to be living together in the intimacy of the married life and for one of them to have entered through faith into the knowledge of the deep things of God while the other remains cynical of all moral and spiritual values. In this case they will face the problem of making together the basic decisions of life while they operate from fundamentally different understandings of life's meaning. There are similar adjustments to be made when the man of faith seeks to live in society with those who move in a completely secularized world.

Deeper than the problem of adjustment to those around him, however, is the problem which the man of faith faces when he seeks to order his own life both by the insights of the Christian faith and by the wisdom of the world. Every educated man who lives in the modern world has in the background of his thinking a vast store of information that has come to him from sources not directly related to the Christian faith. These will include the various branches of learning through which men have sought to understand the nature of the universe. Through such studies as chemistry, physics, biology, geology, and astronomy, the range of human knowledge about the universe has been amazingly extended. Moreover, the modern man has received information about the nature of man and his relationships from the study of history, economics, psychology, and philosophy. The inner problem of the modern Christian is to build for himself a unified philosophy of life in which he combines the insights of the Christian faith with the knowledge of his world received from the vast store of information available to man apart from any concern with religious faith.

This problem which can be brought to a focus in the life of an individual is present with those who would carry on a program of Christian teaching. It would be possible in our church schools to give a type of intensive Bible study which made no effort to see the bearing of biblical truth on the understanding of the world which people have received from the secular society of which they are inevitably a part. This type of Christian teaching, however, would not help people to be vitally related to the world in which they live.

On the other hand, it is obvious that we cannot give in our church schools adequate courses in such studies as chemistry and engineering or even biology and psychology. The Christian educator must seek to help the student face all of his relationships—to God, to himself, to other men, to the natural world, and to history—in the light of the gospel and with the understanding that comes to him from disciplined and fearless study in all areas of human inquiry. This means that he must deal constantly with the relation between truth received by revelation and knowledge gained through the use of his mind.

Concerning the Wisdom of Man

As we seek to see the life of man in the light of God, we must deal with integrity with the various disciplines by which man has come to an increased understanding of the nature of the universe. Each of the areas of man's search for knowledge must be studied with respect for its methods of investigation and with the readiness to listen to what the experts in this field are telling us. We should recognize with gratitude the vast services to mankind which have come from man's increasing mastery of the physical universe. In a manner that probably goes beyond anything contemplated by the author of Genesis, man has entered his earth and subdued it. With the freedom for scientific investigation, there has come the industrial revolution in which man's capacity to produce the goods and services he needs has been vastly increased.

Who can measure the deliverance to mankind that has come through the development of cheap sources of power? We shudder when we think of the galley slaves who were the primary source of power for many of the ships of the ancient world. Who can estimate the impact on modern life of improved methods of transportation and communication? We assume today the telephone, the radio, and the television. The discovery of atomic energy is opening up for our generation undreamed of possibilities for power. Who can fully appreciate the influence of modern medicine on the physical well-being of men today? Modern man owes a great debt to those who have helped him achieve an ever-increasing capacity to use the forces of his universe for his own purposes.

When we consider the progress the human race has made in recent years, we can understand the point of view of those who feel that man's salvation is to come through the development of his material resources. Many of those who are committed to a secular philosophy of life reject the insights of religious faith as irrelevant and as a hindrance to man in his search for a better society. Within a vast portion of our earth, a communist philosophy in which religion is relegated to the realm of superstition is dominant. Even in the Western world a vast secularization of human life has taken place. Great areas of the life of modern man no longer have any vital relation to the insights of the Christian faith.

Along with this secularization of the modern world, there is, of course, a certain uneasiness—a realization that material prosperity does not necessarily mean better living. The various developments of our scientific age are in themselves nonmoral. They can be a blessing or a curse in accordance with the way in which they are used. With the development of the atomic bomb and the weapons of destruction associated with nuclear warfare, the very existence of human life on our planet is endangered. Modern man is no longer certain of his capacity to save himself from the weapons of destruction he has created. The dilemma of modern man is that he lacks the moral and spiritual insights and the resources of spiritual power to control the energies he has released.

CONCERNING THE WISDOM OF GOD

When modern man begins to recognize the limitations of human wisdom, it is proper for him to ask if there is a Word of God which will give him surer guidance as he seeks to understand the meaning of his existence. The dilemma of modern man makes it appropriate to ask if there is truth that has come by revelation. As we face seriously the question of truth through revelation, we turn naturally to the Bible as the book which claims to bear witness to God's revelation of himself to man. But before we seek to hear the message of the Bible for modern man, a word of caution needs to be spoken both to those who deal with the wisdom of man and to those who proclaim the Word of God.

We have insisted that the integrity of the secular approach to knowledge must be protected. We must also insist that those who deal with the various areas of human knowledge must be prepared to recognize the limitations of their approach to reality. It is quite proper for the scientist to say that his study of the physical universe reveals to him a world of law and order that is devoid of any concern for human welfare or for moral and spiritual values. It does not follow, however, that it is impossible to believe in a personal God at the heart of the universe who is interested in every human being. The scientist must assume the dependability of the laws of nature and work on an hypothesis which does not include the concept of miracle. Because the scientist deals only with second causes and not with the ultimate source of life, we cannot conclude from his studies that God is unable to move within the world of nature for the salvation of his people.

A similar word of caution must be spoken to the man who seeks to find the Word of God for our generation in the Scriptures. We who stand within the fellowship of the Christian church believe that the Bible is the Word of God. We believe that the Bible can become an infallible guide for faith and life to those who yield themselves to it. But all that we have said in our second chapter about the human element in the making of the Scriptures must be remembered here. It is easy to confuse the heart of the Bible's message with the thought forms in which this message is expressed. There is history in the Bible, but the Bible is not written to teach history. The statements of historical facts which are found in the Bible must be checked with the knowledge of historical events which have come to us from secular sources if the records of the Bible are to be taken as history. The biblical writers assume the cosmology of their time. We do not have to defend their cosmology in order to hear their witness to God as Creator and their understanding of man as a creature made in the image of God.

When we recognize the importance of knowledge gained through secular sources, we in no way reject the possibility of a knowledge of God that has come to us through revelation. A valid approach to the knowledge of God through the testimony of persons to whom God has made himself known must also be recognized. The Bible is a written document which points beyond itself to the God who has made himself known to man.

We must recognize the vast difference between the assumptions which underlie the Bible and those of the secular world. The writers of the Old Testament do not argue about the reality of the Word of God. They bear witness to the Word which they have received. The difference in basic assumptions between the Bible and the modern world comes to a focus when we face the person of Jesus Christ. Jesus Christ cannot by any stretch of the imagination be made to fit into a pattern which is not offensive to the secular world. In the biblical witness, Jesus is declared to be God manifest in the flesh. He is born of a virgin. He exercises miraculous powers. He is sinless. He dies on the cross and rises again from the dead on the third day. He manifests himself as alive to his disciples over a period of forty days. He ascends into heaven. He pours forth his Spirit on his followers at Pentecost. His followers are conscious of his continuing presence as they bear witness to him to the end of the age. All of these affirmations are alien to the scientific thought forms of the modern world.

The ultimate authority of the Bible is in the power of the risen Lord to speak through the words of the Bible to the needs of men today. Because the Bible moves on a plane that is deeper than that of human wisdom, it is able to point us to the wisdom of God.

The Necessity of Revelation

The writers of the Old Testament recognized the necessity of revelation for a true understanding of the meaning of life. In the book of Proverbs, we read: "Where there is no prophecy the people cast off restraint" (Proverbs 29:18). The Hebrew word which is translated prophecy here could properly be rendered "vision" or "revelation." The writer of Proverbs says that when men have no revelation to guide them they will cast off all restraints.

Jesus affirms the same truth when in the first temptation he quotes from Deuteronomy: "Man shall not live by bread alone, but by every word that proceeds from the mouth of God" (Matthew 4:4; cf. Deuteronomy 8:3). In these words, Jesus ties together the Old and New Testaments. The words were originally spoken to warn the children of Israel against the spiritual dangers involved as they moved from the desert to the richer, more prosperous life of Canaan. Jesus gives them a universal application. In the first place, he says that man cannot live by bread alone. He thus states that secular philosophy is inadequate for the permanent satisfaction of man's life. If man is to achieve the good life, he needs more than the satisfaction of his material needs. Woodrow Wilson spoke to this point when he said: "Our civilization cannot survive materially unless it is redeemed spiritually." He did not say that a material civilization was in need of redemption. This, of course, would be true. Wilson's statement is that the permanent survival of a material civilization is dependent upon its spiritual redemption.

Jesus, however, does more than state that man cannot live by bread alone. He says that the true basis of man's life is the Word of God. It is from the Word of God that man must find the necessary insights to guide him in his earthly existence. The ultimate answers to the questions of human destiny are not and never have been in the flesh. The Bible is the indispensable book for Christian teaching because it is in the Bible and only in the Bible that we have our knowledge of the way God has made himself known to man in history.

The Life of Man in the Light of God

The purpose of Christian teaching is to enable us to see the whole life of man in the light of God. As we approach this task, we must remember that the great insights of biblical faith are never obvious truths which will be understood and accepted by all who are capable of comprehending them. We can prove that the sum of the angles of a triangle is 180 degrees. No one who has any knowledge of geometry will deny this. But we cannot establish in this way the prophetic understanding of history. The great prophets came to their knowledge of God through direct encounter. God had made himself known to them or to their fathers in such a way that they were absolutely certain of his existence, his power, his justice, and his compassion for his people; and because they sought to understand their world with this conception of God, they had to interpret the events of their history in the light of their knowledge of God. Thus, Isaiah could think of Assyria as the rod of the Lord's wrath (Isaiah 10:5). It was from the same point of view that Jeremiah could predict the fall of Jerusalem as an expression of the righteous judgment of God on the sins of his people (Jeremiah 7:1-15).

When we take a long range view of history, we can see the relevance of the prophetic understanding of the history of Israel to the understanding of all history. We may even seek to interpret the rise of Communism in our generation in the same way the prophets interpreted the place of Assyria and Babylon in God's providence. Such an interpretation of history is, however, always a matter of faith—a conviction based on our knowledge of the character of God that must be held in spite of what may at times seem to be massive evidence to support a more materialistic interpretation of history.

Hebrew religion did not begin with the belief that the world was created by God. The Hebrew leaders were driven to their spiritual interpretation of history by the action of God on their lives. The faith of the Hebrews has its roots in the encounter with God in the history of men such as Abraham, Moses, David, Isaiah, and Jeremiah. It was because the Hebrew writers already had a concept of God as he had made himself known to them through the prophets that they were compelled to conceive of the creation in terms of the work of a personal God. In a similar manner, the New Testament writers approached the concept of creation against the background of their overwhelming experience of the God who had made himself known in Jesus Christ. Paul in Colossians says that Jesus "is the image of the invisible God, the first-born of all creation." He goes on to say that "in him [Jesus] all things were created, in heaven and on earth, visible and invisible" (Colossians 1:15-16). These are amazing words to write about a man who had lived in Galilee about a generation before Paul wrote. Paul did not begin with the concept of Creation. His Christian understanding of life began when the risen Lord confronted him on the road to Damascus. When Paul fully understood who Jesus was, it was impossible for him not to think of him also as the Creator. The great insights of biblical faith are never obvious. They involve the understanding of human life that comes when men experience encounter with God. The biblical writers, however, are sure that human life can never be fully understood unless it is seen in the light of God.

Biblical Faith and Human Wisdom

We have defined the task of Christian education as the effort to see all areas of human knowledge in the light of the great insights of biblical faith. It now becomes our task to glance briefly at some of these areas of human knowledge in an effort to see how the wisdom of man must be seen in the light of revelation. The areas which we will consider are simply illustrative of our point of view. This is in no sense intended to be an exhaustive treatment of the subject.

Consider, for example, the world of nature. In the church school we attempt to teach little children that the world of nature is their heavenly Father's world. We speak of the warmth of the sunshine, the beauty of the rose, and the glory of the great out-of-doors. We have had the tendency to ignore the hard and cruel in nature. Yet the very young child can have experiences with poison ivy and mosquitoes. The world of nature revealed in Walt Disney's "Wild Life" series is very different from the understanding of nature that has often been taught in church school lessons. Perhaps our wisest approach is to be realistic in our treatment of the facts of nature and further affirm our confidence that the God who has made himself known by sending his Son to us is also the Lord of nature. Jesus has revealed to us a God who clothes the lilies and has his eye on the sparrows, but he has also revealed a God who is with us in the midst of the storm. Because we believe in the God whom Jesus has revealed, we can see the world of nature in the light of the faith we have received from him and can learn to interpret the deep mystery of pain and death in the light of his cross and resurrection.

Consider from this same point of view our understanding of human nature and human destiny. We can learn much about the life of man from various sources of human knowledge. The story of man's achievements upon our planet is indeed an amazing story. Yet there are insights concerning human nature which come to us only from biblical faith. It is there that we learn that man is a being created in the image of God. It is in the Bible that we see the sin of man as a rebellion against his creator. It is also in the Bible that we see man—sinning man—as loved of God and redeemed by God. It is in the Bible that each individual man learns of the love of God which has come to him in Jesus Christ. In the message of the gospel, man receives the hope of eternal salvation. The biblical understanding of man gives worth and dignity to every human being. The biblical understanding of man as a being created in the image of God with the possibility of an eternal destiny is essential to any adequate understanding of the life of man and his destiny on our planet.

As part of our understanding of man, we must consider the Christian teaching in which each man is told that he must love his neighbor as himself. Due to our rapid advances in transportation and communication, the world is becoming a great community in which it is impossible for people to continue to live in isolation from each other. At the same time, the complexity of our modern civilization makes it increasingly difficult to love or to find the proper expressions of love for all people. In such a world it is desperately important for people to learn the art of living together in peace. The insights of the Christian faith *must* guide us as we seek to grow in our understanding of human relations.

We can see the relevance of the Christian faith to all of life as we consider the Christian stewardship of possessions. Through its development of sources of power and through its mechanization of industry, the modern world has developed an amazing capacity to produce the material goods necessary for the life of man. It is only through the development of the Christian stewardship of possessions that men will be led to use the wealth at their disposal for the good of mankind. The charge to the rich man which Paul gives in 1 Timothy 6:17-19 is meaningless unless the rich man has in common with Paul the basic presuppositions of the Christian faith.

In the tentative design for the curriculum of Christian Education of the Cooperative Curriculum Project, sponsored by a number of Protestant denominations, we find the following statement, "As man responds to God in faith and love, he finds that light is thrown on all of his relationships. Light is thrown on his relationship with God, the sovereign Creator, Father, Redeemer, Judge, so that man may relate to him as a faithful and obedient son. Light is thrown on man's relationship with man (himself and others in society—family, community, world), so that he may relate to man as he was created, in the image of God, as he is, sinner, and as he may become, redeemed. Light is thrown on man's relationship with nature, created and sustained by God to be ruled over, cared for, and used by man as a steward, so that he may relate to nature as the setting in which God has created man to live. Light is thrown on his relationship with history, ruled and overruled by the sovereign Lord, moving forward toward his designed consummation of it, so that man may relate to history as the continuum of God's activity and the temporal aspect of man's response to God's activity." (Pages 10-11 of a document prepared for a meeting of the Cooperative Curriculum Project, December 12-14, St. Louis, Missouri.)

Life's Ultimate Questions

We have been thinking of the relevance of the wisdom of God to the wisdom of man. We have sought to see the whole life of man in the light of God. We have discovered that the wisdom of man must be integrated and interpreted in the light of God's wisdom. It remains to be said that in life's ultimate questions man is dependent entirely on the truth that has come through revelation. This is true as we face the basic question of the existence of God. We can argue for this along the lines of natural theology, and we may or we may not be convinced by this approach. If, however, we are to believe in the God of infinite love who has come to us at great cost to himself, we must listen to those who have seen the light of the knowledge of God's glory in the face of Jesus Christ. It may be difficult to continue belief in the God and Father of our Lord Jesus Christ as we face all of the facts of our human existence. Yet Paul could write: "He who did not spare his own Son but gave him up for us all, will he not also give us all things with him?" (Romans 8:32.) It was in their understanding of the death and resurrection of Jesus Christ that the New Testament writers came to their tremendous certainty of the reality of God.

Through the encounter with God to which the writers of the Bible point, we come to the certainty of a moral absolute. Biblical faith lifts the question of truth above the question of expediency and gives us a moral absolute, a law of the Lord which we cannot violate with impunity. Where the foundations of biblical faith have been rejected, men have no sure basis for an ethic which rises above the level of expediency.

Henry C. Link in his *The Return to Religion* discusses the dilemma of parents who without the benefit of religious faith are trying to pass on to their children the understanding of the eternal distinction between good and evil which they had received from their parents. In this setting he writes: "Those parents who wondered how, in the absence of the religious influences which had moulded them, they could mould the moral habits of their children, were facing an unanswerable problem. *There is no rational substitute for the supernatural power which the unquestioned belief in a Divine Being and a Divine moral order confers."* (Henry C. Link, *The Return to Religion,* p. 104. New York: The Macmillan Company, 1936. Italics mine.)

As we think of life's ultimates, we must remember that all of our human life is marked by existence unto death. Every human being is moving toward the grave, and the wisdom of man has not been able to throw much light on the question of life after death. It is in the resurrection of Christ that we have assured knowledge of the existence of the resurrection world of God, and it is from him that we have the hope of laying hold of an eternal salvation in this life. The Bible is the indispensable Book because it speaks to our human need in its answers to those ultimate questions which can never be answered in the wisdom of man.

QUESTIONS

1. Why is it necessary for each individual to build for himself a unified philosophy in which he understands the wisdom of man in the light of the wisdom of God?
2. Why must the Christian teacher refuse to be satisfied with an exposition of Scripture that avoids coming to grips with the crucial issues of life today?
3. What should be the attitude of the Christian teacher toward knowledge that has come to us from secular sources?
4. What do we mean when we say that Christian education must respect the integrity of the various areas of human knowledge?
5. How has human life today been enriched by the knowledge that has come from the wisdom of man?
6. What are some of the dangers involved in the discovery of atomic energy?
7. Why is it that we can neither deny nor affirm the existence of God through the investigations of science?
8. Why is it that the figure of Jesus found in the New Testament does not fit into the thought processes of our secularized world?
9. What does Jesus say is the true basis upon which the life of man must be built?

10. Why is it that the great insights of biblical faith are never obvious?

11. What is the impact of the wisdom of God on our understanding of the world of nature? of the nature and destiny of man? of a man's stewardship of his possessions?

12. What light does the Christian witness to Jesus Christ throw on the mystery of death?

VI

Hearing the Word of the Lord

A Philosophy of Christian Communication

THE BIBLE is the indispensable book because it gives knowledge of God's revelation of himself to man. The Bible is the indispensable book because the life of man can be understood only as it is seen in the light of God. However, when we have asserted in the strongest terms the significance of the Bible to man's need, we are still faced with the question of how the message of the Bible can be made relevant to the life of the world today. The Bible is the Word of God for man, but faith comes by hearing. Men must hear the message that God speaks through the Bible if the Word of God is to have power in their lives. Our purpose in this chapter is to set forth some of the principles that will be helpful to those who are called to teach the Bible in our day. How can we accord the Bible its proper place in the teaching ministry of the church? How can we give our witness to its meaning and create the setting in which the Holy Spirit can bring its message home to the life of the learner?

THE WITNESS OF THE NEW TESTAMENT CHURCH—OUR CLUE

Communication in the New Testament Church

Perhaps the best way for us to be true to the Bible in our teaching ministry today is to go back to the New Testament church to discover the distinctive marks of its witness. If we had asked the first followers of Jesus how the message entrusted to them was to be communicated, we would have received from them a clear and unqualified answer. The apostles knew that Jesus had given them the obligation of witnessing to the things they had seen and heard. Luke tells us that the risen Lord said to them: "Thus it is written, that the Christ should suffer and on the third day rise from the dead, and that repentance and forgiveness of sins should be preached in his name to all nations, beginning at Jerusalem. *You are witnesses of these things.* And behold, I send the promise of my Father upon you; but stay in the city, until you are clothed with power from on high" (Luke 24:46-49). Luke also says that Jesus said to his disciples: "You shall receive power when the Holy Spirit has come upon you; and *you shall be my witnesses* in Jerusalem and in all Judea and Samaria and to the end of the earth (Acts 1:8). Peter in his sermon on the day of Pentecost says: "This Jesus God raised up, and of that *we all are witnesses*" (Acts 2:32). When Peter and John were charged by the Sanhedrin "not to speak or teach at all in the name of Jesus," they replied, "whether it is right in the sight of God to listen to you rather than to God, you must judge; for *we cannot but speak of what we have seen and heard*" (Acts 4:19). When Peter spoke to those who were assembled at the home of Cornelius in Caesarea, he said: "God raised him [Jesus] on the third day and made him manifest; not to all the people but to us *who were chosen by God as witnesses,* who ate and drank with him after he rose from the dead" (Acts 10:40-41).

Marks of the New Testament Witness

The witness of the first Christians to Jesus was given in many places and was expressed in many different ways, but it always included certain common elements.

1. The message of these Christians always set forth their testimony to that which God had done in Christ. They told of the life and death and resurrection of Jesus. They came to the hearer with a piece of news about an event that had taken place in history—a piece of news to which the hearer must give attention.

2. The testimony of the New Testament Christians always comes out of the community of faith and calls man into the community of faith. It is the voice of those who have become aware of God's disclosure of himself in Jesus Christ and have responded

to him in faith, love, and obedience; it calls for response on the part of the listener. It is the affirmation of those who through their response have been drawn by God into a new community. In the fourth chapter of Acts we have, verses 32-37, a description of the company of those who believed. They "were of one heart and one soul . . . and great grace was upon them all." In this setting we are told that "with great power the apostles gave their testimony to the resurrection of the Lord Jesus." The testimony to the Resurrection becomes believable when it proceeds from a transformed community, and it becomes significant to the hearer when he, in turn, is ready to identify himself with the community.

3. The New Testament preachers always gave the significance of the events connected with Christ's coming as they were understood within the Christian community. The death and resurrection of Jesus were not presented as isolated events but as an integral part of the work of redemption which God had wrought out for the salvation of man. There was of course no uncertainty about the objective truth of this understanding of the events of revelation. These Christians were sure that the Son of God had loved them and had given himself for them (Galatians 2:20). They were equally certain that God had brought him again from the dead . . . "by the blood of the eternal covenant" (Hebrews 13:20).

4. The New Testament witness to Jesus was always given in its bearing on the Christian way of life. The apostles never failed to bring home to their hearers the implications of their testimony for the lives of those who were in their audience. Early Christian preaching had a disturbing way of putting those who heard it in the place of decision. In his first sermon, Peter asked all who heard him to repent and be baptized in the name of Jesus Christ for the forgiveness of sins (Acts 2:38). John wrote his Gospel in the hope that those who read it would believe in Jesus as the Christ, the Son of God, and that believing they would have life in his name (John 20:31). No man ever heard Paul speak of Jesus Christ without facing the necessity of decision. The call to faith was always the call to love and obedience. It was the call to the way of life that Jesus had shown to his disciples.

Those who had known Jesus in the flesh and had been witnesses of his resurrection were under a tremendous sense of urgency as they sought to tell others what they had seen and heard. We feel the compulsion of the witness who must speak when we read the opening verses of the first letter of John as he says: "That which was from the beginning, which we have heard, which we have seen with our eyes, which we have looked upon and touched with our hands, concerning the word of life—the life was made manifest, and we saw it, and testify to it, and proclaim to you the eternal life which was with the Father and was made manifest to us—that which we have seen and heard we proclaim also to you, so that you may have fellowship with us; and our fellowship is with the Father and with his Son Jesus Christ" (1 John 1:1-3). The testimony of these Christians was given in obedience to a divine command and in the hope of bringing those who heard it into fellowship with the Father and with his Son Jesus Christ.

Witnesses Once Removed

When this testimony was heard and believed, it put those who had received it under the same compulsion to witness which the first disciples had known. Much of the writing of the New Testament comes to us from those who were, in a sense, second generation Christians. These Christians had not seen the risen Lord, but they were part of the community of those who believed the witness of the apostles. The writer of the letter to the Hebrews belongs to those who may be called witnesses once-removed. He does not write as an eyewitness but he does write as one who has known those who have known the Lord. He tells us this in his second chapter as he says: "How shall we escape if we neglect such a great salvation? It was declared at first by the Lord, *and it was attested to us by those who heard him,* while God also bore witness by signs and wonders and various miracles and by gifts of the Holy Spirit distributed according to his own will" (Hebrews 2:3-4). Here we have the witness of those who had heard the Lord and the confirmation of that witness in the activity of God within the Christian community. We notice also in the opening sentence of this quotation a sense of urgency and understanding of the necessity of decision on the part of those who hear the witness to the Lord. The writer begins by asking the question: "How shall we escape if we neglect such a great salvation?"

When we listen to the testimony of the Scripture writers, we are but one step removed from the testimony of those who were chosen of God to be actual witnesses to Jesus Christ. When we listen to the testimony of the biblical writers, centuries fall away and we are in the presence of those who must point to the disclosure of God given in Jesus Christ. When we read the New Testament, we hear the words of those who have seen the risen Lord. Jesus in his words to Thomas has placed his blessing on "those who have not seen and yet believe" (John 20:29).

THE PRESENCE OF THE RISEN LORD

The testimony of the first Christians was based upon the assumption of his unseen but real presence. Jesus promises his presence to his disciples in the commission given to the eleven disciples in Galilee. He says to them: "Go therefore and make disciples of all nations, baptizing them in the name of the Father and of the Son and of the Holy Spirit, teaching them to observe all that I have commanded you; and *lo, I am with you always,* to the close of the age" (Matthew 28:19-20). The reference to the close of the age means that this promise continues until Christ returns.

The promise of the presence of the risen Lord with his disciples cannot be separated from the promise of the witness of the Holy Spirit. The promise is given in Acts when the risen Lord says to his disciples: "You shall receive power when the Holy Spirit has come upon you; and you shall be my witnesses in Jerusalem and in all Judea and Samaria and to the end of the earth" (Acts 1:8).

The witness of the first disciples was given on the assumption that if they would be faithful in their witness to what God had done in Christ, the Lord himself would authenticate his message in the hearts of the hearers. These Christians were called to a seemingly impossible task. They were to announce that God had manifested himself in the flesh. They were to point to a crucified Jew as the Son of God. They were to give their witness to the resurrection of Jesus Christ from the dead. They were to ask of men a surrender to Jesus as Lord which made deep and far-reaching demands on those who responded. They were to seek to see the meaning of the whole of our human existence in the light of the knowledge of God's glory which they had seen in Jesus Christ. The story which the first Christians had to tell was a fantastic story, and we are not surprised to learn that to most Jews it was offense and that to many Greeks it was foolishness. The witness of the first Christians was to events that were alien to the thought forms of either ancient or modern man.

The simple fact was that God honored the witness of these first Christians by using it to call the Christian church into being. The preaching of the apostles on the day of Pentecost was accompanied by the witness of the Holy Spirit in the hearts of those who heard it. The response on the part of the people of Jerusalem meant that a believing community was to be found in the city in which Jesus had been crucified. In a few years there appeared in many centers of the Roman Empire a church which was the pillar and ground of the truth.

Consider in this connection the story of the conversion of Lydia. Paul and his companions were strangers in the city of Philippi. As far as we know, the message of the gospel had never been preached on the continent of Europe. Paul took advantage of an opportunity to speak to a group of women who were gathered by the river for prayer. Luke tells us that the *Lord opened the heart of Lydia to attend to the things which were spoken by Paul* (Acts 16:14).

Consider from the same point of view the story of the establishment of the church at Thessalonica. Paul and his companions came to Thessalonica after they had been driven out of Berea. As he had opportunity, Paul preached in Thessalonica a message which he was sure was the Word of God. As Paul writes to the Thessalonians of this experience he says: "We also thank God constantly for this, that when you received the word of God which you heard from us, you accepted it not as the word of men but as what it really is, the word of God, which is at work in you believers" (1 Thessalonians 2:13). In the first chapter, as Paul seeks to account for the acceptance of his message by the Thessalonians as the Word of God, he writes: "We know, brethren beloved by God, that he has chosen you; for our gospel came to you not only in word, but also in power and *in the Holy Spirit and with full conviction.*"

The New Testament witness to Jesus Christ was given by men who knew that they were frail and sinning men. These men knew also that the Christ had sent them as his messengers to bear his name "before the Gentiles and kings and the sons of Israel" (Acts 9:15). The testimony of these first Christians was given in the expectancy that the Lord would speak through them and authenticate his message to those who heard them. God used the witness of these men to call unto himself a people to be the instrument of his redemptive purpose for all mankind.

A similar process takes place today when the men of our generation hear in the Scriptures the witness of the apostles and the first disciples to Jesus Christ. When the living Christ makes himself known to men through the testimony which they have found in the Scriptures, he calls them into the fellowship of his church and lays upon them the responsibility of witnessing concerning him to their own contemporaries. This witness, like the witness of the New Testament, must be offered by frail and sinning men in the hope that the living Lord will honor it as the medium of his message to men today.

A Limitation and a Hope

The understanding of the nature of the Christian witness, which we have set forth here, marks the limits within which we must operate as we seek to bring the Bible's message to bear on the life of the world today. At the same time, it sets forth the hope that is always present as men seek to interpret the message of the Bible. The limitation is found in the fact that all effective Christian communication comes as the activity of God himself. We cannot manipulate the work of the Holy Spirit. We cannot control the time or the place or the means through which the living Lord may choose to make himself known. But the hope which must be present in all Christian preaching and teaching is the hope that God will see fit to use our human efforts as the medium through which he confronts men and women today. The hope is that God through our witness will continually call his church into being. The hope is that God will use us as the bearer of his word to our generation.

Although one generation cannot slavishly imitate another, it may be that the elements that marked the witness of the New Testament Christians can furnish us with a clue concerning the characteristics which will make our witness worthy of the message which it carries. Is it not possible for us to test the methods employed for the communication of the biblical message today by the four elements which we have discerned as the marks of New Testament communication? Should not Christian witness today always include: (1) testimony to what God has done, (2) identification with the church of Jesus Christ, (3) interpretation of the significance of the message to our own day, and (4) challenge to obedience to the living Lord of the church? These four elements of the New Testament witness can assist us in shaping our own witness to what God has done and will do.

THE SETTINGS IN WHICH THE WITNESS MAY TAKE PLACE

Our consistent purpose, as we give our Christian witness today, is to present the Bible's message in such a manner that the hearer will become aware of God's disclosure of himself in Jesus Christ and will respond in faith, love, and obedience to it. As we examine the contemporary scene, we can distinguish at least four settings in which the Christian witness may effectively take place. We shall think successively of the place of the Bible in the life of the gathered congregation, in the Christian home, in the life of the individual, and in the systematic study of the church. These are not all of the possible settings nor are they mutually exclusive. They do give a pattern in which we can consider the place of the Bible in various aspects of the life of the Christian community. As Christian communication takes place in each of these settings, it should be marked by those features characteristic of Christian communication in the New Testament. We will carry on the stream of witnessing to the world of God's redemptive love in every setting in which Christian communication takes place (1) if we proclaim what God has done in Christ, (2) if we make our witness from the community of faith urging the listener to participate with us in the community of faith, (3) if we make clear the significance of the events to our own lives and urge the listener to seek their significance for him, and (4) if we move with the listener in obedience to the word in whatever it may require. These four elements should mark our witness whenever and however it is made if we are to carry on our witness in the tradition of the New Testament church.

THE WORD OF GOD TO THE GATHERED CONGREGATION

Central to the life of God's people is the gathering together of the congregation for the worship of God. There are many elements in this aspect of the life of the Christian community. Of great importance among these is the nonverbal communication which takes place when people find themselves a part of the worshiping community. This aspect is particularly essential in the experiences of young children. Who can overestimate the significance in the children's lives of their joining with parents and other adults in the public worship of God? We cannot treat exhaustively all that is involved when the people of God gather for worship, but we can consider the place of the Scriptures in the various parts of public worship.

The Sermon. The proclamation of the Word of God in the sermon has always been at the heart of Christian communication. We may distinguish three forms of the Word of God. They are the Word of God in the sermon, the Word of God in the Scriptures, and the Word of God in the revelation events to which the Scriptures point. The written Word stands between the revelation event and the Christian proclamation which takes place in the sermon. In the sermon, the minister seeks to make a biblical truth relevant to his people. This means that the minister proclaims the story of redemption as he finds it in the written Word. He does not seek to give to the congregation his own opinions. Instead, he seeks to enter into the meaning of the Scripture's message as a member of the community of faith and to become the bearer of this message to his congregation. In his effort to proclaim God's Word in the passage before him, the minister must bring to his study all of the necessary disciplines of heart and mind. It must be his purpose to point out for his people the significance of the message for their lives. The message which he proclaims from the pulpit must be commissioned speech. He must utter as the spokesman of God the message of the Gospel. He must pronounce the word of judgment and give the call to repentance. He must speak as the bearer of the word of forgiveness to those who are willing to receive it. He must call to decision. And his preaching, like the preaching of the New Testament, must be based on the assumption that the living Lord is present to authenticate the word of his messenger. "It is the presence of the risen Christ that makes a human witness a real witness." (Dietrich Ritschl, *A Theology of Proclamation,* page 61. Richmond: John Knox Press, 1960.) In the life of a congregation there is no substitute for the faithful proclamation of the Bible's message by a minister whom God has called to be the bearer of his word.

Christian preaching is never the isolated act of the minister. It is Christian proclamation in which the hearer who is not a Christian finds himself inevitably involved in lines of spiritual empathy between preacher and congregation. Dr. Donald G. Miller in his book, *Fire in Thy Mouth,* illustrates this element of Christian preaching in the following paragraph. He writes: "Sienkiewicz . . . in his *Quo Vadis?* . . . pictures a young Roman, Vinicius, who, in love with a beautiful Christian girl who has spurned his love because he is a pagan and has fled from him, goes in search of her to a secret night gathering of Christians for worship in the Ostrianum, a Roman cemetery. Sitting there incognito, a pagan in a Christian worship service, he hears Peter preach and is caught up into the sphere of spiritual influence created by the response of the group to the preaching. How does this affect him? 'He felt,' says the writer, 'that if he wished . . . to follow that teaching, he would have to place on a burning pile all his thoughts, habits, and character, his whole nature up to that moment, burn them into ashes, and then fill himself with a life altogether different, and an entirely new soul.' *That is what preaching is designed to do,* and would do far more often in our day if the conditions for doing it were created by the preaching of the minister and the response of the gathered congregation." (*Fire in Thy Mouth,* pages 130-131. Nashville: Abingdon Press, 1954.)

Reading the Bible. The understanding of the Word of God in the sermon is vital to Christian proclamation. There is also a proper place in Christian worship for reading aloud the written word to the gathered congregation. Paul wrote to Timothy: "Till I come, attend to the public reading of scripture, to preaching, to teaching" (1 Timothy 4:13). In this way he emphasizes the significance of the public reading of the Scriptures in the worship of the early Christians. It was and continues to be the best way of making known to them the events through which God had come to man. We need to realize, of course, that probably many of these Christians could not read and that many of those who could read probably did not have Bibles. Apart from this obvious need for reading the written Word aloud, there was a distinct value in the way the Christians gathered together to read from the Book which contained the written record of the revelation which God had given to his people. It provided a means by which the congregation could identify itself with the people and the events through which God had made himself known. The Christians soon began to add to the writings which we now call the Old Testament other writings which had come out of the life and witness of the Christian community. Paul tells the Colossians to read the letter he has written to Laodicea and to see that the letter written to the Colossians was read also in the church of the Laodiceans (Colossians 4:16). The public reading of the Scriptures to the assembled congregation can be the means which God uses to bring home the message of the Bible to those gathered together to worship him.

Christian Hymns. In the written record of Israel's faith the Psalms occupy a unique place. They affirm the witness of Israel to the mighty acts of her God. In these affirmations the response of Israel to the revelation of her God is given. In Psalm 103, for example, we have the statement that the Lord "made known his ways to Moses, his acts to the people of Israel" (verse 7). The Psalm as a whole is deeply devotional poetry in which the psalmist calls upon his soul to bless the Lord and to "forget not all his benefits." The Psalms give effective witness to Israel's understanding of her faith. At the same time, they are effective instruments for the proclamation of this faith.

A similar significance should be given to the Christian hymns. The beginnings of this are in the New Testament. When Paul is writing to Timothy, he refers to the great mystery which is at the heart of the Christian faith. He proceeds to define this mystery by quoting words which are probably taken from a very ancient Christian hymn. He points to a unique Person who has appeared in history as he says:

> He was manifested in the flesh,
> vindicated in the Spirit,
> seen by angels,
> preached among the nations,
> believed on in the world,
> taken up in glory.
> (1 Timothy 3:16.)

We should notice that the first two and the last of these six statements are affirmations of fact concerning the One who has come to us. Paul points to a supernatural Person who was manifested in the flesh, vindicated in the Spirit, and taken up into glory. The remaining three give the response to this Person. He was seen by angels, he was preached among the nations, he was believed on in the world. In this arrangement of the passage, we move from the Person whom God has sent to the church which he has called into being as the pillar and ground of the truth. The singing of hymns such as this fragment which has been preserved for us must have been a most effective way for the first Christians to witness and to invite others to join them.

The selection of hymns for Christian worship today should be made on the basis of the four elements which we have discovered in the witness of the New Testament church. The hymns should proclaim the story of redemption. They should invite participation with the people of God; they should make clear the deep significance of the gospel for the one who sings; and they should send him out in obedience to undertake the living of the Christian life. The hymns should give the great affirmations of the Christian faith and interpret their significance for the people of God. They should call men to decision and obedience. Christian hymns should present the biblical message in its witness to Jesus Christ. They should be instruments through which the living Lord confronts men today.

Public Prayer. As we think of the worship of the assembled congregation as a means of witness, we should not neglect the place of public prayer. It is in public prayer that an individual acts as the spokesman of the congregation as he presents to God the praises and the petitions of his people. Public prayer is based on the assumption of the Lord's presence with the congregation. We cannot manipulate the sense of the presence of God, but it is in public prayer that the consciousness of the reality of the presence of God is most apt to be felt. It is as the congregation waits for the moving of the Spirit of God that a context is created which is appropriate for the mystery of man's encounter with the living God.

The Impact of Christian Worship. Paul, in his first letter to the Corinthians, pictures an unbeliever who has found himself in the midst of the Christian community at Corinth when this community is gathered together for witness and worship. The type of worship which Paul clearly has in mind is an informal service in which the Christians share with each other various elements of their Christian experience. As he thinks of the impact of this service on the unbeliever, Paul insists that the various parts of the service shall be done decently and in order. He is convinced, however, that the effect of the service upon the unbeliever should be that "he is convicted by all, he is called to account by all, the secrets of his heart are disclosed; and so, falling on his face, he will worship God and declare that God is really among you" (1 Corinthians 14:24-25). The worship of the congregation should always recall the story of God's mighty acts, call the worshiper to identification with the people of God, make plain the significance of God's revelation for our own lives, and urge us to obedience to his holy will.

The Word of God in the Christian Home

We have thought of the message of the Bible as it is given to the assembled congregation. Christians today should heed the New Testament injunction not to forsake the assembling of themselves together (Hebrews 10:25). The message of the Bible is mediated through the sermon, through the public reading of the Scriptures, through the singing of Christian hymns, and through participation in public prayer. The emphasis upon the public worship of God should not, however, cause us to neglect the place of the Bible in the Christian home.

When we think of the life of the Christian home, we should realize that with very young children much of the Bible's message will be shared through nonverbal communication. The child of Christian parents is from the very beginning set in the context of a family life which is part of the life of God's people. The child experiences in the home such things as acceptance as he is, the knowledge that he is wanted and needed, justice that sets standards of right and wrong, the forgiveness that continues to accept him even when he has done wrong, and the respect for truth as God's demand on his people. The child who has known love and acceptance in a truly Christian home is prepared to pass from his relationships at home to the knowledge of God's love which will be with him in all of life. While the emphasis on nonverbal communication is particularly important as we deal with young children, it continues with us at every stage of human development. Parents will teach more by what they are and by what they do than by what they say.

The knowledge of the importance of the home's atmosphere does not excuse parents from the conscious effort to communicate the Bible's message to their children verbally. We must realize that the Bible is basically an adult book and that a greater understanding of its significance will come as the child enters into maturity. But there are many things that parents can do to help prepare their children for the understanding of the message of the Bible. Before the children are old enough to understand much of the biblical content they can be led to understand that the Bible is the book to which the adults at home go for their knowledge of God and for their understanding of his will for them. The very small child can begin to realize that the Bible is the Word of God and the source of the faith that gives meaning to his parents' lives.

The security of the home presents the ideal setting in which to tell the great stories of the Bible as part of the spiritual heritage of God's people. These stories can serve as the family's proclamation of what God has done. The stories should be told without moralizing and with no attempt to hold up the biblical characters as perfect examples of what Christians today should seek to become. The biblical stories, if properly told, can lead children to an awareness of the way God has made himself known in the history of his people. The relating of these stories can prepare the way for the child's understanding of the significance of these stories for him and his response to the demands of God on his own life.

The home also gives an effective setting for situational teaching. As children begin to ask questions, parents can answer many of them on the basis of their knowledge of the teaching of the Bible. Jesus did some of his most effective teaching as he used the situation he faced to lead men to the understanding of God's will for them.

There should be a place within the life of the home for the reading of the Scriptures as a part of family worship. The details of the way in which this is done must be worked out in accordance with the schedule of the home, the age of the children, and the possibility of freedom from interruption. In the past, the family altar in the Christian home has been one of the most effective means of communicating the Christian faith. After his description of Bible reading as part of family worship in the home of the Scottish peasant, Burns wrote:

> From scenes like these old Scotia's grandeur springs,
> That makes her loved at home, revered abroad.
> (The Cotter's Saturday Night.)

The home is probably the most appropriate place for the memorizing of passages of Scripture and for explaining and memorizing catechisms which summarize the message of the Bible.

Christians in the United States of America live in a world in which there is freedom of assembly for public worship and freedom for the church to carry on a teaching ministry in the church school. We should give thanks for these freedoms that are part of our spiritual heritage. We need, however, to remember that in lands in which the Christian church has been persecuted, Christians have not always enjoyed such freedoms. In societies in which the Christians have been a persecuted minority, it has often been necessary for the message of the Bible to be transmitted from one generation to another through the teaching of the faith within the home. It is within the life of the Christian home that children should be led to become aware of the meaning for them of the faith which is a rightful heritage from their parents. The involvement of the child in the total life of the home should inevitably lead to his involvement with the faith that has created the spiritual atmosphere of his home. The goal of all Christian teaching within the home is achieved when the faith of the parents comes alive in the lives of the children.

The Bible in the Life of the Individual

We have thought of the place of the Bible in the public worship of God and in the life of the home. It is important also for us to think of the Bible's place in the devotional life of the individual. The various emphases support each other. Parents are not apt to give the Bible a significant place in the life of the home if they have not learned to read it in their own devotional life. The worship of the family needs to be enriched by the worship which takes place within the gathered congregation. The disciplined study of the Bible by individuals is of crucial importance if the message of the Bible is to be mediated to the world today. We refer here both to the private study of the Bible and to the reading of the Bible in the devotional life of the individual. The life of faith must be nourished by the Scriptures.

As men have read the Bible in the expectancy of hearing from it the Word of the Lord, some of the great beginnings of Christian history have taken place. We are thinking in particular of what happened to Augustine when he was led to take the Bible and read it. We would remember also the way Luther was led through his study of Galatians and Romans to the rediscovery of the Pauline doctrine of salvation by faith alone and to the laying of the foundations of the Protestant Reformation.

The world is familiar with the story of the way Alexander Smith, the last male survivor of the Bounty mutineers on Pitcairns' Island, discovered a copy of the Bible in a chest of one of the sailors. At the time, he represented the sole link between the little isolated community on the island and the heritage of his past. His ability to read was limited, but he made his way painfully through the Bible beginning with the Old Testament. As he was reading the New Testament, he came to a vital faith in Jesus Christ. He made confession of his sins and felt that he had received forgiveness for them. He broke with his evil past and began to live as a child of God. As soon as he had passed through this experience of conversion, he began to feel his responsibility for the women and children on the island. He began teaching them to read. He became the teacher of the Bible to a community that for eighteen years had no contact with the outside world. The impact of the message of the Bible on the life of the community was revolutionary. A community which had been properly described as a bit of hell on earth became a reverent and God-fearing community. Through their contact with this one copy of the Bible, the people of this community came to the knowledge of that which God had done for them in Jesus Christ and to the hope of an eternal salvation.

A similar story has come out of the experience of the American soldiers on Okinawa. The soldiers found a village in which the whole level of life was different from that found in other villages in the area. On investigation they found that no missionary had ever worked in the village. The transformation of the village had taken place because two men from the village had brought back from a trip a copy of the Bible that they could read. They had read it and responded to its message and taught it to the people of the village. Through this one Book the people of the village had come to the knowledge of God's disclosure of himself in Jesus Christ. As they had responded in faith, love, and obedience, the life of the village had been changed.

Several years ago I heard a Baptist minister, who at the time was pastor of a church in Washington, D. C., tell the story of an experience he had had in his own congregation. Among those who attended his church was a brilliant scientist who confessed to this minister that he was lacking in any positive faith. The minister asked the scientist if he would be willing for two weeks to try the experiment of getting up in the middle of the night, when nothing would disturb him, and meditating for an hour on the Gospel of John. The scientist agreed to this and faithfully took an hour each night to listen to John's witness to Jesus Christ. At first it was merely an experience of listening and waiting, but soon he found that he began to become involved in the things that John was saying. At the end of the period, he came to his pastor and told him that things which he had not believed were possible had happened to him as he had taken time to be alone with the Bible and to wait for the God of the Bible to make himself known to him. In this experience the scientist passed through doubt to a life of faith. Later he left Washington to teach in a university. After a few years the minister who told this story was invited to speak in a Religious Emphasis Week in this university. He learned from the President of the University that the invitation had been extended to him at the suggestion of the scientist who had formerly been a member of his church. The President of the University told the minister that this scientist was the most influential man on the university campus in his witness to the students concerning the meaning of a vital faith in Jesus Christ.*

In the devotional life of the individual, when a man takes time to be alone with the Bible and to open his life to its message, the experience of encounter with God most frequently takes place. God can authenticate his Word to those who are willing to hear

* This story was told anonymously. I heard it at a meeting of the Richmond Ministerial Association. I give it here without identifying the minister who told it.

it. As the living Lord confronts individuals through the written Word, the life of the church is continually renewed.

THE BIBLE IN THE SYSTEMATIC STUDY OF THE CHURCH

We have thought of the ways the church today can bear witness to God's mighty acts through the sermon and congregational worship. We have considered also the place of the Bible in the life of the Christian home and the way the living Lord speaks through the Bible to the life of the individual. Now it is our purpose to consider the place of the Bible in the systematic study of the church. Christians should be prepared to give serious study to the effort to understand their faith. It has been said of the early Christians that they out-thought, out-lived, and out-died the pagan world. While no one would underestimate the importance of the last two of these achievements, our concern here is with the first. Christians should know the firm foundations of their faith in the mighty acts of God. They should know the implications of their faith as they are spelled out in the church's doctrine. They should see these doctrines in their relation to each other and as they stand together to form a systematic whole setting forth an understanding of our human existence that has unity and integrity. They must face the task of seeing every aspect of man's life as it is to be understood in the light of the gospel. We have the beginnings of this task in the New Testament. In Romans, Paul points to the God who did not spare his own Son but gave him up for us all (Romans 8:32). In the opening chapter, he paints in the darkest terms the sin of man apart from Christ. He knows that God has predestined those whom he has called to be conformed to the image of his Son. He sees the created universe as sharing in the bondage of corruption and waiting for the redemption of the sons of God. He spells out in the twelfth chapter some of the implications of the Christian's faith for Christian living. The letter to the Romans is a penetrating statement of the meaning of the Christian faith which was designed to enable the Christians at Rome to stand firm in the midst of many adversaries.

Christians should be prepared to give to the study of the Bible the same kind of disciplined effort that men give to the mastery of the secular disciplines. No one would expect to understand physics or engineering without serious effort. It is imperative that Christians today be willing to pay the price of serious study as they seek to understand the Bible's message. In the sections that follow, we will suggest some approaches to and some methods of Bible study. These could properly be considered as part of our treatment of the Bible's place in the systematic study of the church. They are closely related to the consideration of this theme. Since these suggestions will apply also to the place of the Bible in the other settings we have considered, we will develop them as separate topics.

APPROACHES TO BIBLE STUDY

From Scripture to Life

There are two generally recognized approaches to Bible study. We can start with a passage of Scripture and concentrate on its meaning until we feel that we understand the message which the writer meant to convey to his readers. We can meditate on the passage in the hope that God will speak his Word to us through it. When we feel we have adequately entered into the meaning of the passage, we can seek to understand its relevancy to us and to the life of our world. The strength of this type of Bible study is that it involves the student in the careful study of the text of Scripture. Its obvious weakness is that all too often the student fails to follow through to a clear understanding of the implication of biblical truth for life today.

From Life to Scripture

We can approach the study of the Scripture from our knowledge of the needs of persons. We can seek to understand the needs of persons at the various age levels and to move from this knowledge to the discovery of the answer to these needs which are found in the Scripture. This is a fruitful approach to the study of the Bible. It is the approach of the seeker after truth rather than that of the detached spectator. The questions that we bring to the

Bible will do much to determine our capacity to hear its message. The approach from the needs of growing persons to the understanding of the message of Scripture has resulted in a greatly enriched teaching ministry in Protestant religious education. There are, however, some dangers in the "need" approach to Scripture which should be guarded against. This type of Bible study can be based on a shallow and inadequate understanding of the dimensions of human need, and the kind of questions asked may limit the kind of answers found. The full depth of our human need is seen only when the life of man is seen in the light of God. This type of Bible study can make the mistake of assuming that the answers of the Scripture to the needs of human life are so obvious that they can be found without serious study of the text of Scripture. The strength of this approach is that it is consistently in vital contact with the needs of persons.

The two approaches to Bible study are not necessarily contradictory. In Christian education as a whole, we are returning to a strong emphasis on content. The Bible contains a record of factual information. We must grasp the facts of the Bible in their relation to each other before we can evaluate the relevance of these facts for life today. Biblical teaching is concerned with the story of what God has done, but it must never be *purely* concerned with telling the story. The ability to name in succession the kings of Israel and Judah does not mean that the student has understood the prophetic interpretation of this period in the history of God's people. From the other point of view, the study of the Bible should never consist merely in asking questions. It is important for us to ask the right questions, but we must not be like the American tourists who ask many questions but never stay for an answer. We must linger with the Bible until we have received *its* answers to *our* questions.

THE ONE STORY OF THE BIBLE

There is a third significant approach to Bible study. We must always seek to hear the one story of the Bible which underlies all of its varied narratives. The Bible must be consistently understood as the written witness to the revelation of God in the history of a particular people, Israel. When we enter deeply into the meaning of the story which the Bible has to tell, we must understand that the central actor is God himself. It is the action of God which gives unity to the book as a whole. The Bible is not so much the story of man's quest for God as it is witness to God's quest for man. The book of Genesis must be understood as the story of the discipline through which God prepared a holy family to be the instrument of his redemptive purpose. The narrative of the events of the Exodus must be understood as Israel's witness to the way the Lord brought her up out of the land of Egypt, out of the house of bondage. The story of the wandering in the wilderness and the account of the conquest of the land of Canaan must be seen in the same perspective. The long history of Israel in the promised land must be seen as the setting in which God makes himself known in the life of a people. The significance of the great prophets of Israel is that they appear as spokesman for the Lord. The destruction of the kingdoms of Israel and Judah should be seen with prophetic insight as an encounter of these peoples with their God. Underlying the whole of the story of this peculiar people is the biblical emphasis on the faithfulness of God in spite of the faithlessness of men.

When we come to the New Testament, we find the same story moving on to its conclusion. We are filled with supreme wonder at the coming of God to man in the Incarnation. We need to understand the life, death, and resurrection of Jesus Christ as the consummation of revelation. We need to bow in reverence before the supreme mystery of a redemption wrought out both for Jews and Gentiles. We need to see in the church, the Israel of God, the new community through which God sends his offer of salvation to all mankind. We need to see the continuity between this community and the church today. We have not understood the Bible if we have failed to see the one story which underlies the many stories.

Book Studies

There is a proper place in the study of the Bible as a whole for the concentration on the intensive study of special books of the

Bible. This kind of study should never be undertaken in isolation from the study of the rest of the Bible. We should seek to understand each book in its place in the movement of the Bible as a whole. We should be ready at all times to supplement and support ideas which have come to us from the study of one book with the results of the study of other books. Still one of the most fruitful approaches to Bible study is to concentrate on the study of a book. When we study intensively the message of a book of the Bible, we are most apt to come to the place at which the fundamental biblical concepts emerge and confront us in our own life situations.

CHARACTER STUDIES

Another valid approach to an understanding of the Bible is through the study of the characters of the Bible. As we study the personalities of the Bible, we are dealing not with the creations of a mythology but with real men and women who had to make their decisions and live their lives in the setting of the life situations in which they found themselves. In their assumptions concerning the nature of the universe in which they live, the biblical characters differ widely from each other and even more widely from the people of the twentieth century. The common element between the personalities of the Bible and the people of today is that the God who made himself known to the men and women of the Bible is the God who has come to us in Jesus Christ and the God who confronts us in our life situations today. When we see the people of the Bible in their encounter with God, we prepare the way for the encounter with God which we may experience today.

METHODS OF BIBLE STUDY

We have thought of the various approaches to Bible study. We can move from the study of the Bible to the understanding of its relevance to life. We can move from the need of man to the message of the Scriptures. In either case, we must be aware of the one story of the Bible with its witness to God's activity in calling into being the redemptive community through which he seeks to call all men to become his children. The study of the approaches to Bible study leads naturally to the consideration of methods of Bible study.

The Lecture Method

There is a proper place in the systematic study of the church for the use of the lecture method. When this method is used, the teacher makes a careful study of the passage which is being considered and seeks to open its meaning to the group he is teaching. Much that has been said about the relation of the sermon to the written word applies also to this type of biblical teaching. The purpose of the teacher is not to present his own ideas but to hear the message of the passage he is teaching and to communicate to his class the message he has received. In his study, the teacher should consult commentaries that give the background of the Scripture and discuss the meaning of the words, the structure of the sentences, etc. For this type of study, a knowledge of the original languages is helpful, but the aids to Bible study which are available in English are so adequate that the consecrated teacher who is limited to English can do a remarkable job of entering into the meaning of the Scripture.

If the lecture method is used, it is usually more effective when combined with other methods. For example, opportunity for questions and discussion may be given at the end of the lecture. "Listening teams" may be chosen before the lecture and asked to listen for and to report on certain things which are presented in the talk. Visual aids of many kinds may be used along with the lecture. Panels may be asked to react to what the speaker has said. Various devices may be used before the lecture to create an atmosphere of expectancy. In these and other ways an atmosphere of group involvement can be created.

The final test of the effectiveness of the lecture method in Bible teaching is the capacity of the teacher to help his class become involved in the full implications of the biblical material he is presenting. In effective biblical teaching there must be an interplay between the teacher and the class in which they stimulate each other and come to the point at which they seek together to become the hearers of the Word of the Lord.

We should understand also that the lecture method, while suitable at times in the teaching of adults, is not used with children. The teacher of children should have a thorough understanding of a Bible passage so that she can teach from the overflow, but she will have to teach with methods which are suitable for her age group.

GROUP BIBLE STUDY

While the lecture method has a place in Bible teaching, it is effective only when it is used by a competent teacher. It has often become a dry as dust monologue in which the group has a minimum of participation. The tendency in adult work today is toward a type of Bible study in which groups seek to study the Bible together. This method of study may take many forms. The group may depend on a leader to open up the study and guide the discussion without dominating it, or the individual members of the group may study carefully the passage to be considered and come together to share with each other the results of their study. In the give and take of such a discussion, the various members of the group will stimulate one another. In this type of teaching there can be opportunities for breaking up large classes into small groups to consider various aspects of a problem which is being studied. The reports of these groups can be evaluated by the class as a whole. Such a procedure brings a maximum of class participation in discussion and evaluation.

At other times, various points of view may be presented by such devices as role playing. Different members of the class may seek to enter sympathetically into the understanding of different positions. In still other situations, the dramatization of the biblical narrative may become an effective way of participating in the story. The playing of Bible stories is a fruitful method of familiarizing people with these stories and of helping them to identify themselves with God's people. When group Bible study is carried on with an understanding of the various processes of group dynamics, it may be possible to come to a group consciousness in which the impact of the biblical message becomes vital in the whole life of the group.

The advantages of this type of approach for the enrichment of

Bible teaching are obvious. We should realize, however, that in group Bible study we cannot afford to dispense with the disciplines involved in individual study of the Scripture. Unless serious effort is made to hear the message of the Scripture, group Bible study can degenerate into reading into Scripture the prejudices of the group. When a group of people unite to study the Scriptures under the guidance of the Holy Spirit with the willingness to move out in obedience to the leading of the Spirit, the great biblical ideas can emerge in power to confront and transform human life. We cannot control the exprience of encounter, but we can say that the way is prepared for the living Lord to make himself known when a group of people give themselves to the serious study of the Bible in the hope that God will speak his word to them through the Bible.

Telling the Bible Stories

The telling of Bible stories is an important method for the communication of biblical truth to all age groups. The Bible contains perhaps the greatest collection of stories known to the human race. As people have read the Bible, the knowledge of these stories has entered into the very structure of society. These stories are about real people who actually lived at various times in the history of God's people. These stories give accounts of events that actually happened at different times and places in human history. The biblical stories are a significant part of the spiritual heritage of the people of God. They tell of what men and women did to each other. Underlying all of them there is a dimension of depth because the central actor is God himself. It is this that distinguishes the biblical stories from the great stories of the Greeks and the Romans. In the telling of the biblical story in Christian teaching, it is essential for us not to lose the witness of the story to the activity of God. We must not humanize these stories in order to make them move in the thought patterns of the modern world. If we consistently take the supernatural element out of the biblical stories, we have made many of them insipid and meaningless. We must not distort the biblical stories to suit our preconceived ideas of the way the events of biblical history must have happened. A story of Jesus devoid of all supernatural elements would bear little resemblance to the memory of the Christ which was preserved for us by the first Christians. We must not remove from the biblical stories the elements of mystery and wonder and awe which are appropriate to man the creature when confronted by the supreme mystery of God's revelation of himself.

We must not distort the biblical stories. Yet Christian teachers should tell them with a clear understanding of the capacity of the children at the various age levels to receive them. There are biblical stories which are appropriate for the teaching of Juniors that would be meaningless to Kindergarten children. Some stories which are rich in meaning for adults would be out of place for Juniors. Teachers who understand the capacities of children should select the stories of the Bible which they feel are suitable for the children they teach. The probability is that the range of these stories could be greatly increased if we told them as part of the heritage of the people of God and not to moralize about various aspects of children's conduct.

MEMORIZING THE BIBLE

There is a place in the systematic study of the church for the memorizing of Scripture. We need to commit the words of the Scripture to memory so that we can have them available as part of our inner resources. The verses of the Bible which we seek to memorize should be verses which have meaning to us. This does not mean that we must understand the full meaning of a passage of Scripture before we commit it to memory. A child can memorize from the fourteenth chapter of John the request of Philip: "Lord, show us the Father, and we shall be satisfied," and the answer of Jesus: "Have I been with you so long, and yet you do not know me, Philip? He who has seen me has seen the Father" (John 14:8-9). The child can understand something of Philip's desire for a vision of the Father in heaven. He can understand also a part of what Jesus means when he says: "He who has seen me has seen the Father." As he grows in maturity, he will still find that the language he has learned expresses a deepening faith. Adults who have meditated profoundly into the meaning of the

Christian faith will not have fathomed the full meaning of that statement of Jesus: "He who has seen me has seen the Father."

The child can memorize Ephesians 4:32, which reads: "Be kind to one another, tenderhearted, forgiving one another, as God in Christ forgave you." The child can understand that Christians should be kind to one another. He can dimly feel that Christians forgive one another because they know that God in Christ has forgiven them. Mature Christians can quote this verse from Ephesians with an ever-deepening sense of its meaning. The passages of the Scripture which we seek to memorize should be graded to the capacities of children at the various age levels. Here also we must not avoid verses that include elements of wonder and awe. Who can fail to feel the wonder of John's statements: "In the beginning was the Word, and the Word was with God, and the Word was God. . . . And the Word became flesh and dwelt among us, full of grace and truth; we have beheld his glory, glory as of the only Son from the Father" (John 1:1, 14).

We forget the things we have memorized that are meaningless to us, but we will frequently recall the things that express, better than we ourselves can express them, our deepest feelings and our strongest convictions. The great passages of the Bible which we have committed to memory may become a rich part of our spiritual resources. The Word of God which we have stored in our hearts may become the medium through which the Holy Spirit speaks to us in our time of need.

Creeds and Catechisms

We should seek always in Bible study to come to a correct understanding of the meaning of the passage which is before us. When this has been done, we cannot avoid the necessity of trying to relate the truths we have learned from different passages to each other. We need to work toward an ordered and unified understanding of the message of the Bible as a whole. In the long run we cannot avoid seeking to relate the truths which we have received from the Bible to our understanding of the whole range of our human existence.

As we seek to organize and unify our knowledge of the Bible

we feel the need for becoming familiar with the creeds and catechisms of the church. The creeds are attempts of other Christians who have listened to the message of the Scripture to express in an ordered and systematic form their understanding of the message of the Bible. The catechisms express in the form of questions and answers the questions which other men have put to the Scriptures and the answers they have received. If the student of the Bible can understand the questions of the catechisms as his questions, he is prepare to listen to the answers. If the catechism asks the right questions, i.e., the questions which men must inevitably ask as they seek to understand the Scriptures, its answers can guide the student as he seeks to find the answers to his own questions. From this point of view, the question, What is justification?, in the Westminster Shorter Catechism can be discovered as a classic statement of the way in which the leaders of the Protestant Reformation answered the question of how sinning man could be made right with God. (Question 33 in the Westminster Shorter Catechism). If an individual is familiar with the questions and answers of the catechisms, he may find that through these answers he can give expression to his own faith.

We must never forget that the creeds are confessions of faith that have been wrought out in the midst of controversy. Through them men have confessed their faith and have taken their stand for convictions that were meaningful to them. When men give expression to their faith through the historic creeds of the church, they are giving their Christian witness to that which God has done for them in Jesus Christ. The creeds are human documents which seek to give expression to the truth that has come through the self-disclosure of God which is witnessed to in the written Word. As the church confesses her faith through her creeds, she gives a witness which the living Lord can honor as he confronts men today.

We started in this chapter with the question of how the message of the Bible could be made relevant to the life of man today. We have walked a long road as we have looked at various aspects of the teaching ministry of the church. As we bring this study of how we can communicate the Bible message to a close, we are reminded of a passage from the Apostle Paul as he describes the sense of urgency with which he sought to communicate the message of the gospel to his own contemporaries. He writes: "Though I am free from all men, I have made myself a slave to all, that I might win the more. To the Jews I became as a Jew, in order to win Jews; to those under the law I became as one under the law—though not being myself under the law—that I might win those under the law. To those outside the law I became as one outside the law—not being without law toward God but under the law of Christ—that I might win those outside the law. To the weak I became weak, that I might win the weak. I have become all things to all men, that I might by all means save some" (1 Corinthians 9:19-22). In his passion to get his message into the hearts of men and win them to Jesus Christ, Paul was ready to do anything that he could, short of the compromise of the truth, to reach men for God. Those who teach the Bible today must share Paul's passion and be ready to use every legitimate means at their disposal to bring the message of the Scripture to bear on the need of man today. They must do this in the hope that the living Lord will honor their efforts as he confronts men and women today with his demands on their lives.

Questions

1. Why is the question of method crucial as we face the problem of bringing the message of the Bible to bear on the life of the world today?
2. What are the assumptions underlying the command to witness to him which Jesus gave to his disciples?
3. What is the note of urgency which we find in the witness of the first disciples to Jesus Christ?
4. How is it that through the reading of the Bible today we become "witnesses once removed" from the first witness to Jesus?
5. How does the existence of the Christian church show that the expectation of the witness of the first disciples was fulfilled?
6. Read 1 Corinthians 15:1-11. What does it mean to you if you believe Paul's statement in verse 8?
7. How would you define the hope that underlies the Christian witness today? What are the limitations within which the Christian witness must always operate?
8. What is the peculiar place of the sermon in the proclamation of the Word of God? How is the expectation of the Word of God in the sermon supported by the public worship of the gathered congregation?

9. Can you give some examples drawn from your own experience or the experiences of your friends of the way in which the living Lord has made himself known to individuals through their Bible study?

10. What in your opinion is the place of the Christian home in the communication of the message of the Bible?

11. What are the elements of strength and weakness in the attempt to move from the study of a passage of Scripture to the understanding of its relevance to life?

12. Why is it important at times for us to move from our knowledge of human need to the study of the answer to this need as it is found in the Bible? What are the dangers to be guarded against in this type of approach?

13. Why is it essential for our understanding for us to know the *one* story of the Bible?

14. What are the advantages and disadvantages of the lecture method of Bible study?

15. What is the strength of the group approach to Bible study?

16. What are some of the principles which would guide you in the selection of Bible stories to tell to children?

17. How does the study of the characters of the Bible prepare the way for encounter with God today?

18. Think over the things which you memorized years ago that you still remember. Why have you not forgotten them? How have they served to enrich your life? What do your answers to these questions say to you about memorizing the Bible?

19. List some of the basic questions concerning the meaning and purpose of life that you would like to have answered. Can you find these questions or questions similar to them in the Westminster Shorter Catechism? How do the answers in the catechism compare with the answers you would have given to your questions?

20. What is the place of the creeds in summarizing the results of Bible study?

21. What different methods of Bible study would you like to experiment with in your private study of the Bible and in your Bible teaching?